The Best of Engle's Angle

A Humorous Slant on Life and our Wacky World

KEVIN S. ENGLE

ISBN: 1544749589
ISBN 13: 9781544749587
Library of Congress Control Number: 2017904451
CreateSpace Independent Publishing Platform
North Charleston, South Carolina

Since this is my first book, I think it's only appropriate that I dedicate it to my first wife Judy.

In fact, she's my current wife, as of today, and I'm hoping she'll stick around for a while longer.

If there's a second book, well, we'll cross that bridge when we get to it. ☺

TABLE OF CONTENTS

ACKNOWLEDGEMENTS

To Dan McDermott, Publisher and Editor-in-Chief of the *Warren County Report/Frederick County Report* for printing my articles these past 10 years. I appreciate it.

To Marlene A. and Marlene E. Dee. Cousin Phil. Ron S. and Mary T. Your encouraging and supportive words over the years have meant more to me than you'll ever know. They've inspired me to keep doing this. Thank you.

And to my wife Judy for nudging me, and sometimes pushing, ☺, to make this book a reality. We did it.

INTRODUCTION

"What do you want to do when you grow up?"

I never liked that question. Probably because I never had a good answer for it. I'm still not sure I do, but at some point, I stumbled upon the realization I like to write. I only wish I would've figured that out years ago. But hey, that's life isn't it?

It's hard for me to believe I've been creating my *Engle's Angle* columns for 10 years. Wow. The ones in this book were reader favorites, as well as some of my own.

I hope you'll enjoy reading them, whether it's the first time or you've seen them before.

If you keep reading, I'll keep writing.

Deal?

Kevin

PART ONE

OK, I'm Strange

AH, NO THANKS

"Don't shake my hand. Don't shake my hand. Please don't shake my hand."

That's what goes through my head when I walk into church and see her standing there. It's not that I don't like the white-haired woman handing out bulletins. I don't even know her. She's probably a very nice lady. What I do know is that she just blew her nose and hasn't had a chance to wash her hands. As nice as she probably is, I'd rather not shake her hand until she washed it. She gives me a bulletin and says hello. And then sticks out her right hand to greet me.

Hmmm.

As I'm sitting in church thinking about that germ exchange, I see the minister blow his nose. Ok, what's going on here? Unless he leaves during the service, he won't be washing his hands either. Guess who's breaking the communion bread in a few minutes and giving it to everyone?

I'm not feeling too well.

Communion at my church is a germ fest. We do it by intinction. That's a fancy word that means the minister breaks off a chunk of bread and gives it to me. This is the same guy who just blew his nose. I take that piece of bread and dip it in the communion cup. More often than not, grape juice isn't the only thing in that cup. Take a peek and you'll see other chunks of bread floating along. How they got there I'm not sure, but they're there. Some folks like to eat their grape juice-soaked bread directly over the cup. How nice. That brings to mind all sorts of unpleasant thoughts.

My brother was visiting when the subject of intinction came up. He won't do it. He's a smart guy.

There's a saying that cleanliness is next to godliness. I don't think the people in my church are familiar with it.

Sunday service ends and I head for the door. The minister is already standing there, greeting worshippers as they leave. Here we go again.

"Don't shake my hand. Don't shake my hand. Please don't shake my hand."

"Have a good week," he tells me and smiles. And then sticks out his hand.

ORDER, SHIP, TRACK, TRACK, TRACK

My wife and I are trackers. She's the backwoods kind. I'm your 21st century variety.

She can look at animal prints in the yard or on the driveway and know who or what they belong to.

"You see that?" she'll say as her finger carefully traces the outline of a hoof print. "That's a reindeer."

"A reindeer?"

"Yup. And those lines in the snow? Up on the roof?"

The ones I didn't even notice.

"Looks like a sleigh to me."

I don't track reindeer, or sleighs. I track packages. I like to order stuff on line, and then track it as it makes its way to my door.

And that's why the holidays are my favorite time of year. Lots of stuff to track. I'll buy stuff for my wife. I'll buy stuff for me. I'll buy stuff just to buy stuff. Just so I can track it.

I'll go on line several times a day, copying and pasting those 25 digit tracking numbers into the shipper's website just so I can see where my package is at that very moment. I even have a map of the U.S. on my wall that I mark with the current location of all my orders. It's like having my very own Santa GPS.

I get excited when I read the words 'Origin Scan', 'In Transit', and my favorite, 'Out for Delivery'.

For me, tracking packages is more exciting than getting packages.

"Your stuff is in St. Louis," I'll tell my wife. "It should be here Saturday. And those pears we love? We'll be eating one tomorrow."

She just gives me that look.

But that's ok. I know I'm weird.

With all the hustle and bustle of the holidays, sometimes I'm up for a little competition. And that's when I'll order stuff from two different companies on the same day, just to see which gets here faster.

And who doesn't like getting things early?

Me.

Getting a package a day early means one less day to track it. One less day of excitement.

"I don't want it Wednesday!" I'll tell the company. "I want it Thursday. The day it's supposed to be here."

If it does arrive early, there's really only one way to get over the disappointment. Buy something else and start over.

My biggest thrill is looking outside and seeing that delivery truck pull up the driveway. I run to the window and watch as the driver emerges from the truck holding my box. The box I've been following all the way from Lexington to Roanoke to right here.

And when he sets it by the door?

It doesn't get any better than that.

"Welcome home package," I'll say as I wipe away a tear. "Welcome home."

■ ■ ■

The author tracked his wife's flight the other day. From El Paso to Denver to Dulles airport. And next time, maybe she'll bring him something.

CHEWERS AND CHOMPERS

I like yogurt.

My wife's not a big fan, nor does she like to be around me when I'm eating it.

She says I chew my yogurt.

Ok, maybe I do.

What's the big deal?

Isn't that what you're supposed to do with your food?

Isn't that why we have teeth?

According to her, and probably most people, there are certain foods you don't need to chew. Yogurt is one of them.

"You just smush it around in your mouth and then swallow," she says. "No chewing necessary."

Ok, maybe so, but in my defense, it's a soft chew, not a hard one. I do the same thing with pudding and oatmeal.

There's no question what you're supposed to do with chewing gum. It's right there in the name.

My wife doesn't care.

She's not a gum chewer and doesn't like to be within earshot of me when I'm working on a piece.

She says I go a little crazy with it. Chew a little too loud.

Guilty. Although I don't make those annoying smacking and popping sounds that some people do.

Maybe all this extra chewing is why I've been having issues with my jaw lately. I've been working it too hard all these years.

But I'm not the only one. There are others like me.

I know. I've heard them.

We were eating dinner with a group of people when I heard something, but couldn't figure out what it was.

I kept listening and eventually followed the sound to the other side of the table, zooming in on the source.

The person was a chomper. Her jaws made a clicking sound as she chomped on her food. It sounded like she was in a fight, destroying and pulverizing dinner with her teeth. No doubt she was winning.

I must say it was distracting.

"Did you hear that?" I asked my wife later that night.

"No."

"You're kidding? How couldn't you? That was loud. I don't even do that. Do I?"

She just looked at me.

I'm fairly certain I don't.

My dentist gave me a custom fit mouth guard to wear at night to help with my jaw issues. I asked him if he could see any extra wear and tear on my teeth. Maybe all this extra chewing was wearing them down.

He said no.

That's a good thing.

At lunch today, when I eat my smooth style strawberry yogurt, I may try that smushing thing. We'll see.

And the next time I have ice cream? Certainly I don't chew ice cream do I?

Come on, get serious.

■ ■ ■

The author started early. He was born with all his teeth and chewed his baby food.

GUILTY PLEASURES

I did something yesterday I'm not proud of.

Something I shouldn't have.

They say confession is good for the soul.

We'll see.

I was unfaithful to my wife.

But I have a good excuse.

I couldn't help myself!

I'd been thinking about it for some time.

Ever since I read the email.

And yesterday, on a Tuesday afternoon, in a moment of weakness, I gave in to my desires.

I tried to fight it, but it was no use.

She was beautiful.

Hot.

And steamy.

I couldn't say no.

I'm just a guy.

And yes, it was fantastic.

Everything I thought it would be.

It was … delicious.

The best pizza I've had in some time.

I never get pizza on a Tuesday.

We get it on Friday.

It's our thing.

A way to celebrate the start of the weekend.

But they kept sending me emails.

Midweek special. Only $7.99 for a large three topping pizza pie.

The pictures were tempting.

I wanted it.

How could I say no?

Turns out, I couldn't.

I was doing errands.

I was feeling frisky.

Why not?

I deserve it.

It'd been too long.

A week and a half.

When it comes to pizza, that's too long.

I convinced myself it was only a business transaction. Nothing more.

Money exchanged hands. A credit card actually.

I'm ashamed to say it, but afterwards, I didn't even feel guilty.

Not at first anyway.

After all, my wife does it at work every so often.

Why shouldn't I?

But should I tell her?

She'd never find out.

She didn't have to know.

When she came home, I was nervous. On edge.

She sensed it.

I had to come clean.

I had to bare my soul.

I opened the refrigerator door and pointed to the cardboard box.

"How could you?"

"I'm sorry."

A tear rolled down my cheek.

I begged for forgiveness.

I promised I'd never do it again.

And I won't.

I'll never get another luscious, mouth-watering mid-week pizza, no matter how hot and steamy it is.

No matter how many emails they send.

No matter how tempting the photos.

I'll be strong.

I do have to go out again tomorrow.

I'll be near the Dairy Queen®.

Hmmm.

■ ■ ■

After 625 pizzas and a couple hundred DQ® Blizzards® later, happy 25th anniversary Judy.

A REAL LIFE MINION

As a little kid, Halloween never did it for me. Between the store-bought costume with the chintzy mask and the rubber band strapped around my head, and the fact that I wasn't a big candy eater, I never got too excited about it.

And so, at the age of eight, I hung up my Spiderman costume for the last time.

If I did want a piece of candy, my big brother would've shared some of his. After all, he and his friends canvassed the neighborhood with pillow cases to collect all their free booty. There was enough for me too.

Today, some forty plus years later, I'm thinking very seriously about going out on the Trick or Treating trail once again.

Why?

For two reasons.

First of all, I eat a lot more candy now than I did then. I'm not sure what was wrong with me as a kid, but it's now a regular part of my diet. And if I can score some free stuff, why not?

But that's not all. There's another reason, even bigger than free Heath® bars and M&M's®.

I'm in love!

With Minions.

Who couldn't love these adorable little yellow guys dressed in their mini-overalls and goggles? And they're bald, like me.

I don't just love the Minions. I want to be a Minion.

As it turns out, I already am.

According to the picture on the side of the box of Honey Maid crackers I bought at the store, there's Minion Phil and Carl and Stuart and Dave and Jerry, and yes, Kevin. Kevin the Minion.

A few months back, I begged my wife to take me to their movie. How could I not go to a movie where I was one of the stars?

They've been everywhere recently.

On the big screen. In Twinkie boxes. On Amazon boxes. They even have their own cereal.

Some Minions have two eyes, others one. Kevin's got two, like me. He's the tall one with the banana-shaped body.

I was admiring his picture the other day when it hit me.

I own a yellow sweatshirt.

I have a pair of overalls in the closet.

And black shoes and gloves.

And goggles.

I could dress up like a Minion!

I could be Minion Kevin!

And what better time to do it than at Halloween? Sure, people might think I'm weird, but at least I'd have a good excuse.

If a guy in his fifties knocked on your door Halloween night, dressed like a Minion, would you give him some candy?

I'm about to find out!

Trick or Treat!

IT'S ALL IN MY HEAD

I've been feeling sluggish lately. No energy. Tired all the time. My wife says it's because I don't get enough sleep. She's probably right, but I'm guessing mono. Yeah, I'm sure of it. I have mono.

I had my yearly physical last week, complete with blood work. The doctor called a few days later with the results and left a cryptic voice mail message. He suggested I call back and make a follow up appointment. Unfortunately, he won't be back in the office until sometime next week. Great, I've got some rare Amazonian blood disease and there's no cure, I just know it. That's amazing in itself, considering I've never been to the Amazon.

Did I mention I'm somewhat of a hypochondriac? Of course, my wife makes fun of me about it.

"Relax," she says, trying to assure me. And shut me up. "You know your white blood cell count is always low, and you've already been tested for that. I'm sure that's all it is."

"Yeah, you're right," I tell her, just so she won't make fun of me anymore. I bet I won't last another week.

"Ouch," that pain in my tooth is back. I hear root canals aren't very fun.

How soon do you know if you have Lyme's Disease? I'll bet I got it from that tick bite on my leg. And what about West Nile virus? Those mosquitoes looked like they were carriers.

"Whoa, what was that shooting pain in my chest? That didn't feel too nice. Here comes the big one." I always hoped I'd go quick and easy, with no pain. Looks like I'm not going to be so lucky.

And how about all that dust I ate from mulching leaves? That couldn't have been good for the lungs. If the heart attack doesn't do me in, I'd better get an x-ray.

Did I mention I'm a hypochondriac?

My back has been awfully sore for the past two months. I think it's our mattress. My wife says it's my chair at work. Both sound like reasonable explanations, but what my gut is really telling me is that it's some kind of muscular disease. I see a nasty test in my future, complete with long needles.

I'm past due for my annual eye exam. You know, I haven't been seeing as well lately. My wife says it's because I'm getting older. Thanks dear. I think a more likely explanation is because I have some kind of brain tumor that's affecting my retina. That would also explain the headaches.

Great. I have a wart on my finger. Isn't that how those horrible flesh-eating viruses get started?

I can't remember anything anymore. It's probably nothing to worry about. Just early Alzheimer's or maybe dementia.

I'm not feeling so hot. I better lie down for a bit.

THE. LAST. WORD.

E-mail is my preferred method of communication. I don't text. I rarely turn on my cell phone. My Facebook page? I haven't gotten around to that yet. Twitter? Nah. If you want to reach me, call me on the home phone and leave a message, because I'm not that good at answering it, or send me an e-mail.

I think I'm in the minority.

I take that back. I know I'm in the minority.

My best friend from high school typically responds to my e-mails sometime within the calendar year.

"I just haven't gotten into that," he said last time.

Yeah, I kind of picked up on that.

My brother is a little better. He'll get back to me within a few days, but no matter what I ask him, he doesn't say more than a word or two.

Another friend, an eye doctor, isn't the speediest either. Is it really more important to look at people's eyes than to send me a message? Apparently.

My best responder is my cousin. He and I e-mail back and forth frequently, and he's better at keeping up with it than I am.

His messages are always longer than mine. He's a detail kind of guy.

I enjoy reading them, but sometimes, my chin does hit the keyboard as I'm poring over his latest manuscript. Sorry Phil.

He and I play this little game, even though neither of us has acknowledged it.

We both want it.

The.

Last.

Word.

Not in a nasty way.

And we're not trying to outdo each other.

It's just who we are.

We like to dot our I's.

And cross our T's.

We like closure.

If he sends a message, I'll send one back.

And then so will he.

On.

And on.

Neither of us are good at stopping the e-mail chain.

We have to say something.

One.

More.

Thing.

And that's why I have a gazillion messages in my inbox.

But I've decided it's time to change the rules.

It's time to stop 'the Last Word Game'.

Lately, I've been looking for "exit" points. E-mails that I don't really have to respond to, even if I feel I should.

It takes willpower, but I'm learning to hit 'delete' every now and then without replying. By that point, we've already said all we can about whatever the subject happens to be anyway. It's time that e-mail drifted off into space, never to be seen again.

I'm not trying to be rude Phil.
I think you'll understand.
Sound good?
Great.
Ok.
That's it.
Good-bye.
Until next time.
Later.
Out.

the.last.word.the.last.word.the.last.word.

It's best not to argue with people who want the.last.word. It's annoying. Really. Trust me. You get the idea.

WET ONES

As I'm drying my hands, I see it in the bathroom mirror. The big water spot on the front of my pants. Great. Now all my coworkers are going to think I peed myself. What really happened is that I leaned up against the counter and got water on my pants. That's my story and I'm sticking to it.

Don't you hate it when one of your coworkers takes a shower in the sink and gets a little messy? Of course, since it happened at work, this thoughtful person (i.e. slob) assumes that he or she doesn't have to clean it up. And because I didn't remember to look first, I'm now the one with the problem. Isn't that the perfect analogy for work? Someone else messes things up and you have to deal with it.

So now what? I have two choices. Number one. I can wait here until my pants dry, but that could be a while. Plus, there's no place in the bathroom to kill time. I could hand out warm wash cloths like they do in fancy restaurants, but there are no warm wash cloths, only paper towels. Besides, I doubt I'd get any tips. And it would be a little weird.

Number two. Do what I always do in this situation. Head straight for the safety of my cubicle without stopping for anything.

No drink of water, no chit chat, no nothing. My hope is that I don't pass anyone along the way. If I do, I have a plan. Immediately make eye contact and say hello while not stopping for a response. I've got to keep the person's gaze away from my wet zone. If I'm lucky enough to be carrying something, I can strategically place it in front of me as I walk.

Of course, I will pass someone and their eyes will magically drift toward what I don't want them to see. Again, I have options, although not good ones. I can turn around and walk backwards or do pirouettes like a ballet dancer. That way, they'll think I've got bigger problems than water on my pants and will forget all about that wet spot.

Or, I could do the intelligent thing. Stop and tell them exactly what happened, whether I know them or not. We'd share a laugh and then I'd be on my way.

I never do the intelligent thing. Why would I do that?

Why do I even care what others think? I'm a confident, in control, 21st century guy. Little things like water on my pants are only tiny speed bumps on the highway of life. Blink and you're already past them. I know the truth and that's all that matters.

Who am I kidding? I may be a 21st century guy, but I care what other people think about me, and I don't want anyone thinking I peed myself. I'm funny that way.

I could create a diversion like they do in the movies. Maybe set off the fire alarm, but that's illegal, and I don't want to go to jail. Or, I could take a shower in the sink and pour water all over myself. If my pants are already wet, why not all of me?

I pity the person who comes in here next. Poor sucker!

A KEEPER

My wife says I'm a real keeper. I took it as a compliment. You know, like "he's a real catch." Someone you should hang on to. Only trouble is, that's not what she meant.

What she was saying is that I have a habit of keeping things. Things that she doesn't think are worth all that much. And she's right. Stuff like old clothes, old newspapers and junk mail. I've been known to keep socks and underwear with holes in them for long periods of time. To my wife's amazement, or more appropriately, her horror, I even wear them on a regular basis. Sure, if they were cheese, they'd be swiss, but what's a few holes? There's still more than enough material to do the job they were created to do. In other words, they cover and support what they're supposed to. She's assured me on numerous occasions these articles of clothing, if you can still call them that, will soon disappear. I don't actually maintain an inventory, but I'm fairly certain she's not made good on those threats just yet.

Old newspapers. I don't plan on wrapping fish or stuffing them in boxes the next time we move. I keep them because I actually intend to read them. Ok, I admit there are articles that I've never gotten to, including some from five years ago, but they're still on my To Do list. I just need to remember my To Do list.

I don't like to pitch junk mail until after I've looked at it. Why I don't know. Maybe I'm hoping there's a bunch of money in one of those envelopes. I haven't found it yet, but I'm still looking. And when the little piles of junk mail begin to sprout up around the house like weeds, my better half focuses my attention on getting rid of it. And I do.

A few years ago, we did something I don't ever want to do again. Move. Moving is a great time to go through your possessions and toss out what you don't want or know you'll never use again. I did my best, but I have a hard time trashing something if there's even the remotest possibility I might need it some day. I already have plans for several of those nice moving boxes.

I hate to get rid of something even when I don't need it. You know the twisties you get when you buy garbage bags? We have more of those little things than we could ever use in our lifetime, but I just can't bring myself to throw away the new ones. An extra screw or nail? I keep those too, not that I'd know what to do with them. And don't even think about throwing away that tube of toothpaste until you're absolutely certain you've squeezed out every drop.

Ok, I've got a problem, I admit it. But I know where it comes from. My parents. I've come across old greeting cards they kept for years. Birthdays, get well wishes, anniversaries, holidays. You name it, they kept it. I would never do that. That's just silly.

One of my cousins is even worse than me. At least that's what I tell myself. He keeps every credit card receipt and utility bill and neatly stores them away in marked boxes. He's already told his family to pitch them when he kicks the bucket. "Don't even waste your time taking the lids off," he jokes. "Just throw the whole thing away." See, I'm not that bad. I'll bet those boxes could be reused though.

Yeah, I admit it. I'm a keeper. But guess who's a loser? My wife. That's right. She's going to lose her mind living with me. But not to worry, I'll keep it for her.

SANDPAPER AND CELERY

Have you ever wondered what people think about you? You know, what their deep-down-inside true feelings really are?

- A. Sure. Who doesn't?
- B. Maybe. I'm not sure I want to know.
- C. Hell no! I don't give a crap.

If you answered C., you can stop right there. If you said A. or B., here are two ways to find out.

- D. Die
- E. Quit your job.

The bad thing about dying, in addition to the dying part, is that you still won't know because you won't be around to hear it. You can rest in peace, and rest assured, that most likely, people will say nice things to your family, to be polite, unless you really were a jerk.

And for that reason, I chose E.

Ok, let's be honest. I quit my job last year because I didn't like my job. I didn't quit just to find out what people thought about me.

I already knew most of them didn't like me. Ok, let's be brutally honest. None of them liked me.

What I heard during my last two weeks at work were:

F. Some almost nice stuff.
G. A lot of nasty stuff.

"Sorry to see you go," one coworker began.

That sounds like an F.

"but to be honest, I'm glad you're leaving."

That's not very F.

"I never liked you anyway."

Sounds G'ish to me.

"You're like sandpaper," he went on. "Always rubbing me the wrong way."

That's very G.

It was though he was talking *about* me, not *to* me.

"I wish you all the best," said another.

F.

"although," she continued.

Uh oh, that's a G. word.

"I wish it were me instead. I wish I were leaving and you were still here."

That's definitely G.

This went on for a day or two until it finally occurred to me. I won't see most of these people again. Ever. And you know what that means?

It was my turn to go on the offensive. After all, it's better to give than receive right?

"I'm going to miss you," I said to the sandpaper guy.

That's definitely F.

"but not all that much."

G.

"You're like celery," I told him.

F.? G.?

"It's ok," I explained.

F.

"but only in very small quantities."

G.

"after that I can't stand it."

Very G.

And I walked away, feeling good about the conversation. He stood there with a confused look on his face as he compared himself to vegetables.

"I'm glad I met you," I told another.

F.

"because you're the dumbest human being I've ever known. Duh."

G.

"You make my broom look smart."

G.

I should've done this a long time ago. No more hiding behind social correctness.

As I said my final goodbyes to the few people who could actually tolerate me, I got a bit choked up. Of course it was all an act. Sandpaper doesn't cry.

■ ■ ■

Next time, the author will say 'C'.

CUTTING GRASS? NOT BAD.

I like cutting the grass. What I don't like is getting ready to cut the grass. Anymore, it takes just as long.

When I was a kid and it was time to mow the lawn, I'd go outside and mow the lawn. That was it. Not now. It's not that simple anymore. Now, I have to *prepare* to cut the grass before I actually cut the grass. Here's my 10 step pre-grass cutting routine.

Step 1. Put on watch. Not knowing the time is bad. Taking too long to cut the grass, and hence, getting off schedule, is very bad.

Step 2. Put on sunscreen. The sun is bad. You must protect your skin from the sun. Confession … I don't always do that. My wife and my dermatologist tell me that's bad.

Step 3. Put on mask. One of those stupid looking white masks that fits over your nose and mouth and makes it hard to breathe and my glasses to steam up. The ones I used to make fun of when I saw people wearing them. Grass and pollen are bad. Inhaling them is very bad.

Step 4. Put on goggles. Flying objects moving at a high rate of speed are bad. You must protect your eyes from such things. Things like rocks, sticks and acorns.

Step 5. Put on hat. The sun is bad. You must protect your bald head from the sun.

Step 6. Put bug spray all over your body, making certain not to get it in your eyes. Getting bug spray in your eyes is bad.

Step 7. Put on bug net. Annoying gnats that swarm around your face, get in your ears and fly up your nose are extremely bad. You must do anything humanly possible to keep that from happening.

Step 8. Grab a bottle of water. Summer heat and humidity are bad. You must not dehydrate. You must drink liquids. You must not pass out while operating machinery. Doing so is bad.

Step 9. Move 25 things to get the lawn tractor out of the garage. That's annoying, and annoying is bad.

Step 10. Put gas in tank. Running out of gas is bad. Not having enough gas to mow the entire lawn is very bad. Needing to go to the gas station immediately before mowing is bad. Needing to go to the gas station while mowing is criminal. Talk about getting behind schedule.

Ok, I started two hours ago and now it's lunch time. I'm hungry. Cutting the grass while hungry is bad. I'd better go to the bathroom too. Cutting grass with a full bladder is very bad.

IT'S DIRTY OUT THERE

First stop, the dry cleaner. I have a few items to pick up.

I hand the woman behind the counter my credit card and she swipes it through the machine. When the transaction processes, she places my card on the counter.

I wish she wouldn't do that. The counter doesn't look all that clean. Couldn't she just hand it to me?

I pick up the card, wipe it on my pant leg and put it back in my wallet.

Next stop, Lowe's. We need some air filters for the furnace.

As I'm headed to the correct aisle, I spot a penny on the floor. It's my lucky day.

Or is it?

When I bend down to pick it up, something flashes through my brain.

I wonder where it's been?

I already know where it is right now.

On the floor. Where people have been stepping on it for who knows how long.

I hesitate for a second, but pick it up anyway. It may be dirty, but it is money.

Now where do I put it?

Hmm.

I consider my options and shove it in my jeans rear pocket, one that I hardly use.

When I get back to the car, I squirt hand cleaner on my fingers. That should take care of any germs.

Third stop, Costco® Wholesale Club. I'm thinking about joining.

A half hour later, after checking out the place, I'm ready to leave. Before I do, I head to the bathroom.

As I'm taking care of business, my sunglasses case falls out of my jacket and on to the floor.

Wonderful.

You don't want to be dropping anything in a public restroom. They're not always the cleanest places.

When I'm done, I carefully pick up my sunglasses case and head to the sink. I rinse the case with water and then wash my hands. I'll scrub it with cleaner when I get home.

Where do I put it in the car?

Another dilemma.

I stick it on the floor mat. It's dirty too.

Next stop, the library. My cousin suggested a book and I'm looking forward to reading it. I find it and go.

When I pull in my driveway, I stop the car and get the mail out of the box. The gritty grimy mailbox that I only rinse out once or twice a year.

No mail goes upstairs until I've wiped it off in the laundry room. House rule #17.

The next day, while reading the book, I make a discovery. An unpleasant one. There's a dried speck of something stuck to a page.

My best guess? Food of some variety.

Fantastic.

This is exactly why my wife doesn't get books from the library.

I go upstairs to my office and look in the garbage can. The one I only use for 'clean' garbage. No food. I retrieve a piece of paper and go back downstairs where I use it to scrape the dried speck of food into the kitchen garbage can.

I enjoyed the book, but not all of the other discoveries I made while reading it.

Gross.

It's dirty out there folks.

Be careful.

■ ■ ■

The author doesn't think he has OCD, although he may lean in that direction.

THE RULE

Friday. Noon.

"Can I come home now?" I was pleading.

"No! You have errands to do. Get those done and we'll talk about it." My wife can be a real taskmaster.

"But I want to come home."

"Not yet. I'll tell you when it's safe."

One of my favorite times of the week is Friday at lunchtime. That's when I walk out the door at work and start my weekend. But not today. Today is not a regular Friday. Today a contractor is coming to the house to fix some things. And while that's going on, I'm banned from the premises.

Why? Because I'm a neat freak. When I see ladders in the house, I freak out. I don't have anything against ladders, but they're dirty. I don't like dirt. Not in the house anyway.

At our place, we have one big rule. No shoes upstairs. I don't care if the President of the United States pops in for a surprise visit. Those shoes are coming off. Even if I have to wrestle a few Secret Service guys to make it happen.

Not only do the shoes come off, I want you to take them off in a certain place. At the BOTTOM of the basement stairs. Not when you walk in the basement. Not when you're standing outside. At the BOTTOM of the stairs. Got it?

When someone doesn't follow The Rule, I freak out. Sweat runs down my arms while I fixate on the offender's footwear. I can't help it. It's in my DNA.

The good news is Mr. Contractor has been here before. He knows all about The Rule and is good at following it. The bad news? He's bringing a ladder.

Halfway through my errands, I call home.

"Is he there yet?"

"No, he's not coming until tomorrow morning. He got a late start. All's clear."

Saturday. 8AM.

I'm outside. Mr. Contractor should be here any minute. My day's agenda is filled with outside activities. Cut the grass, trim the grass and whatever other yard work that needs done. I might have to mow my neighbors' lawns as well. Whatever it takes.

Noon.

I'm done. He's not.

I'm hungry. My wife and I eat lunch in the basement. That's as far as I'm allowed to go.

A short while later, as I'm pulling weeds, I see something that almost puts me into cardiac arrest. Mr. Contractor steps out on to the porch. The dirty porch. In his socks. And then he goes back inside. In his socks.

A quick recap. Inside. Clean. Outside. Dirty. You don't mix the two.

Ahhhhhhhhhhhhhhhhhhhhhhh!!!

Mid-afternoon.

I'm quickly running out of energy, and enthusiasm. There's more I could do, but I don't feel like it.

Mr. Contractor still hasn't finished. And now he's off to the store to get stuff he needs to complete the job.

A thought crosses my mind. Why not go in and head straight for the shower? That sounds like a good idea. But it's not. In fact, it's a really bad idea. I'd see furniture moved, other stuff out of place, and of course, ladders. I can't do it. I don't do it. I'd have nightmares for sure.

I hop on the exercise bike in the basement and go for a spin. I'm too tired to ride, but I'm running out of ideas.

5PM

Mr. Contractor returns from the store and finishes the job. As soon as he's gone, I'm upstairs. A quick inspection and everything seems to be ok. All is right with the world.

The next day, my wife mentions some other inside projects she'd like done. Projects that require a ladder.

She's obviously not thinking clearly. I need time to recover first.

We can talk about it.

Next year.

PART TWO

To Good Health

AN ANNUAL THING

Remember how much you liked going to the doctor when you were a kid?

Me neither.

Kids don't like going to the doctor.

Adults are the same way. It's not the kind of thing you outgrow. For me, trips to the doctor's office are downright embarrassing.

I go to the dermatologist twice a year. I can get a sunburn in less time that it takes my wife to drink a cup of coffee.

If you've never been to a dermatologist, the routine goes something like this. Take off your clothes and wait for the doctor. Yeah, you can keep your underwear on, and hey, why not put on one of those too small hospital gowns as well. Ok, now sit there and wait. I don't know about you, but I'm not much for sitting around in public places in my underwear. I get a bit self-conscious. And despite a room temperature that's slightly above arctic, I begin to perspire. A lot. When the doctor finally pops in, I'm a puddle of sweat, like Frosty the Snowman when he was trapped in the greenhouse by Professor Hinkle, the evil magician.

Did I mention my doctor is a female? Did I mention how I'm dressed? Geez! She examines me all over. And I do mean all over. Oh boy!

All males, regardless of age, should have certain parts of their anatomy examined each year to make sure all is ok in that neck of the woods. Of course, there's a particular way to dress for this examination. It's called naked. Here go those sweat glands again.

When guys hit 40, the annual physical includes new and wonderful things. The family doctor offers his congratulations on reaching that milestone and promptly rewards us with our first prostate exam.

That's one gift I could do without.

Another new addition to my yearly checkup is the hemoccult test. At least I do this one by myself in my own home, although playing with poop is not a lot of fun no matter where you do it. Yes, the information gained from the test is very important, but getting that information ain't no party. The kit comes with specimen collection paper. Think of it as a close cousin to the seat protectors you find in public restrooms. You're supposed to place the collection paper in the commode and then do your thing. The problem is the paper isn't strong enough to catch anything. As soon as something lands on it, it sinks to the bottom of the commode faster than the Titanic. Because the instructions specifically say to obtain a sample untouched by water, guess what? Better luck next time. When the collection paper is up to the task, it's play time. Grab one of the popsicle sticks, root around a bit and then smear it on the test kit like you were spreading peanut butter on toast. Yeah, it's disgusting. And once isn't enough. You'll need to do this on three separate occasions.

I probably shouldn't complain too much. My wife tells me women don't have it any better.

NO PRESCRIPTION REQUIRED

I was in the drug store the other day. I needed some, well, that's not important.

"It's for a friend of mine," I said to the teenage girl behind the counter, intentionally avoiding all eye contact.

"Uh huh," she said rather unconvincingly, as if she hadn't heard that one before.

I hurriedly put away my wallet and bolted for the door.

She said something as I was almost outside, although I didn't stop to hear what it was.

Drug stores are not for the faint of heart, or those who embarrass easily, like myself. I thought I knew what kind of products they carried, but it wasn't until I took a closer look that I realized there's a lot more on those shelves than aspirin and Band Aids®.

Got ear wax? Then hear this. Head down to your local pharmacy and check out all the removal options available.

How about pain? They got stuff for that too, including some products containing emu oil. I pity the poor emu who *donated* their oil. I'll bet that was painful. Kind of ironic huh? How would you like to be an emu oil extractor? There's a job I wouldn't want.

Flaky, itchy skin? Quit scratching long enough to grab some lotion or ointment.

Feet get big treatment at the pharmacy. If you have bunions, corns, warts, whatever, they have what you need. Are you in the market for an antifungal? Isn't that such a nice sounding name?

One treatment for warts contains propane. That's right. Propane.

"Warning," the label says, "product is highly flammable." If you buy it, I'd strongly recommend keeping a safe distance from any open flames. If you forget that little piece of advice, warts will be the least of your worries.

How about unpleasant odors, whether it's smelly feet, bad breath or just plain ol' gas? Once again, you're in luck. What's more, these products have double benefits. They take care of your problem and make others feel better too.

Got a nasty canker sore in your mouth? That word just sounds bad.

No description of a drug store's merchandise would be complete without mentioning gastrointestinal issues. We've all been there at one time or another. These products come in several categories: can't go, can't stop and can't control.

If you can't go, you've got your laxatives. Just say the word "enema" and I cringe. Can't stop or can't control? They've got what you need.

How about some digestive health prevention? Maybe you've been thinking about a colon cleansing. Then again, maybe not.

Guys, got jock itch? Your favorite cream is available.

Has all of this made you nauseous, like it has me? They got stuff for that as well. The word alone upsets my stomach.

When I got home, it didn't take me long to realize what the clerk was saying as I ran out the door. It seems I forgot something. My purchase. And as soon as my stomach settles down, I'll go back and get it.

TRICK OR TREAT?

"Nah, that couldn't be right. Could it?"

I was on my way to Church on a recent Sunday morning when it caught my eye. Have you ever seen something but didn't quite believe it? That was the case here. I thought I'd read the sign correctly, but I was skeptical.

A few hours later, I remembered it when my wife and I were headed out to lunch.

"Tell me what it says."

"Where is it?"

"On the end. It's bright yellow."

I slowed down as we got closer.

There it was.

"Flu shots!" my wife announced.

Bingo! Exactly what I thought it said.

What's the big deal? Flu shots are a normal thing this time of year.

They are.

What concerned me was where it was.

At the grocery store?

No.

At the drug store?

No.

How about .... the flea market!

Yeah, that's what I thought.

Time out.

Halloween is quickly approaching. The time for ghosts and goblins and other scary things. And there are definitely things in this world that scare me. Like when I'm cruising along on the highway, exceeding the speed limit, and pass a hidden police car. That scares me. Or my mother-in-law's refrigerator. Actually, it's not the refrigerator that scares me. It's what's inside that sends chills up and down my spine. There's stuff in there that hasn't seen the light of day for months.

I can now add another item to my list. Flea market flu shots. That just doesn't sound right.

And it raises a few questions.

First of all, who's giving them? Is it a doctor or nurse trying to make a few extra bucks by setting up shop at the flea market? I have my doubts.

It's probably the same guy who's selling old tires and other junk he's had packed away in his garage for 10 years. Isn't that comforting?

Next question. Where did he get the vaccine? I don't think you can buy them in bulk at Walmart or an online drug store.

And lastly, and most importantly, who's getting their flu shot at the flea market?

Would you?

When I drove by a week later, the sign was even bigger. And scarier.

Buy 1 tire, get a free flu shot.

Buy 2, get your teeth cleaned.

Buy 3 or more, get your eyes checked.

I could only shake my head in amazement. Who would actually do that?

As I walked out of church an hour later, I realized something. My car needed new tires. And I hadn't been to the dentist for some time.

Hmmmmmmmmm.

Trick or treat!

TWICE A YEAR

"Smash, smash, smash!"

No, I'm not watching professional wrestling.

"Silver, silver, silver!"

And it's not a reality show about miners in Alaska.

"Ok, rinse. No food for 30 minutes."

I'm at the dentist. The poor sucker in the chair next to me just had a filling replaced.

And the announcer? That's my dentist. He's been doing play-by-play dentistry for at least 20 years, ever since I've been going to him.

If you were a new patient sitting in the waiting room, you might have second thoughts about walking through that door. And if you heard the following, you'd probably think something else was going on. Something a little more intimate.

"Touching you, touching you!"

Translation – Mr. Dentist is pressing on your tooth.

"I want you, I want you!"

Translation – he's scraping one of your pearly whites, but whatever's on it won't come off.

"Got it!"

Translation – he got it.

My dentist makes me laugh, which is hard to do when I have a dental pick, mirror and suction hose crammed in my mouth.

As a kid, my mother took me to an old German guy with a thick accent who worked on my teeth. I'm fairly certain he had a dental license. Even if he had told me what he was doing, I couldn't have understood him.

When I was a teenager, I wore braces. My orthodontist would tell me what pain he was about to inflict before he did it, but not during. I even named one of his torture tools "the Thumper", a spring-loaded device that I wasn't real fond of.

I've near heard of any other dentists like mine. Where else can you get a dental exam and be entertained all at the same time? It's like a two for one special. I almost look forward to my twice a year appointments.

Almost.

After all, it is the dentist.

"Good, good, good!"

Translation – no cavities.

"You're boring. Get out of here."

Translation – No cavities. See you in six months.

■ ■ ■

Other people tell the author he's boring and they're not even dentists.

WARNING LABELS

After a few weeks of not feeling well, it was time to see the doctor. She said I had a sinus infection and gave me a prescription for it. Like a lot of other things I don't pay attention to, I never read warning labels. For once, I decided I would. I'm glad I did. I think.

Who Should Take This Medication?
Do not give this drug to anyone under 21. Pregnant women should not take it. Women who are not pregnant should also avoid it. Men are advised to stay away from it as well. If you're still foolish enough to try it, the makers of this drug are in no way liable for any side effects you experience, either temporary or permanent. If you bring legal action against us, we'll declare bankruptcy and you'll get squat.

How Should I Take It?
It's up to you. You can take it with food. Or without. You can take it with milk or water. You can take it in the morning, at lunch time or in the evening. It really doesn't matter. The drug has limited effectiveness regardless.

Possible Side Effects
Your teeth may fall out, although this only occurred in nine of ten persons studied. If you have hair, it will probably change colors. For guys, lime green and neon orange are most common. In females, bright pink and purple have shown up more than any other. Six of ten persons experienced rapid hair growth on their ears and nose as well as other places they'd rather not tell you about. You'll be visited by a nasty, itchy rash on various parts of your body. But don't worry, it typically goes away on its own within six to nine months. Definitely no more than a year. Half the people in the clinical trial began talking like a pirate after the first dose, while the other half spoke pig Latin. Everyone developed cravings for lima beans and beet juice. Most persons experienced a sudden and uncontrollable urge to disrobe in public places and sing Elvis songs. We're not sure what that's all about, but you can check out some of the performances on You Tube.

Active Ingredients
None, but amazingly, this drug has still made us a ton of money. As long as people keep taking it, we'll keep making it.

Since I'd already paid for it, I thought I'd give it a try. I'm not feeling any better, but at least I still have my teeth. Most of them anyway.

■ ■ ■

The author is getting used to the orange hair, but isn't too wild about shaving his nose twice a day.

SLIM TO NONE

My wife doesn't like going to the doctor.

I don't like going to the doctor. But if I need to go to the doctor, I do. In fact, I even go sometimes when she thinks I shouldn't. Like a few months back when I felt this bump on the top of my head. For all I knew, it's been there for years. After rubbing it every ten minutes for two days, it was still there. I was concerned. I was worried. Ok, I was obsessed. I made an appointment to see the doctor.

"It's nothing," my wife said.

Of course that's what she said. That's what she always says.

I love my wife. I respect her opinion. But not when it comes to medical advice. She's the last person who would recommend seeing a doctor.

By the day of my appointment, she made me feel guilty for going, like I was being foolish.

I went anyway.

As it turned out, she was right. It was nothing. But hearing that from a doctor, not her, gave me the peace of mind I needed.

Last year, I started seeing these TV commercials talking about shingles and how painful they are. "If you've ever had chicken pox," the commercials said, "the shingles virus is already inside you."

We both had the chicken pox when we were kids. She had them really bad.

"One in three persons will get shingles in their lifetime."

In baseball, that's a good batting average. When it comes to shingles, I didn't like those odds.

I talked to a few people who had them. None of them had nice things to say about the experience. All told stories of painful rashes that took weeks and months to go away.

"Talk to your doctor or pharmacist," the commercials said.

I did. Turns out there's a vaccine. Getting it doesn't mean you won't get shingles, although it reduces your chances by 50%. And if you do get them after having the vaccine, those rashes shouldn't be as bad.

I called our insurance company. It was covered.

Ok, let's review. Shingles, bad. Chances of getting them, decent. Vaccine, good. Cost to me? Nothing.

I got the shot.

And then came the hard part. Convincing my wife to do the same thing.

And that's when the excuses started.

"I don't want to get one during flu season."

And when flu season was over?

"I'm not feeling well. You're not supposed to get the shot if you're sick."

She was right.

But she's better now, after six weeks of coughing and hacking and sneezing and blowing her nose, but of course no trips to the doctor. "He won't give me anything for it," she said.

"What about the side effects?"

"Will you just get the dang shot!" I pleaded.

And last Saturday, she finally did.

By Sunday, her arm was sore. A normal reaction.

By Monday, she had a rash. Again, not that unusual.

By Tuesday, it hurt and kept getting bigger. This isn't good.

"It's the size of a baseball," she said.

She was exaggerating.

Tennis ball maybe, but not a baseball.

She was concerned and so was I. For my own safety. I was afraid she might put a whoopin' on me.

The rash went away a few days later. Thank goodness.

But you can bet I'll be hearing about it for a long time.

■ ■ ■

Mr. Engle's doctor recommended a pneumonia shot. And the likelihood of the Mrs. getting one? How about slim to none.

PART THREE

Life

LEFT OR RIGHT?

I'm tired. It's been a long week. But it's Friday and I'm not at work anymore.

Where I am is at Walmart. Not really where I want to be. I don't have anything against Walmart. I just don't like shopping all that much. But I had to.

As I stand in the aisle, staring at all my choices, my eyes glaze over. My brain feels the same way. I was hoping to grab and go, my preferred method of shopping. Yeah, like that ever happens.

"I remember the day when there was only toothpaste."

"Me too," I said to the guy beside me.

Today isn't that day.

Do I want Tartar control? How about Gum Protection? Or maybe Extra Whitening? Maybe I don't want white teeth. Maybe I'd prefer green or yellow.

Do we really need all these choices? Do people actually buy 47 different kinds of toothpaste? I just want to brush my teeth.

I make my decision. Tartar control, regular flavored.

But not so fast.

One tube or two? I'll save money if I buy the two pack. Being the obsessive-compulsive person I am, I do a quick calculation.

Buying two now will save me 11 cents in the long run. I grab the two pack.

Next item on the list. Dishwasher detergent.

Do I want liquid, gel, granules or these new things that look like hard candy? I wouldn't recommend them though. I tried one and it didn't taste all that good, although it did clean my mouth out. My wife likes them, for cleaning the dishes that is.

Do I get the blue and green ones or the yellow and orange ones? I kind of like the yellow and orange color combo, but we've been using the other ones. I'd better stick with them.

Do I get the 16 pack or do I go all out and buy the bucket of 48? I do another calculation. I grab the bucket. I just saved another 89 cents.

What's next?

A battery for the little clock in the bathroom. It died a few weeks ago. After my wife figured out how to remove it, something that's beyond my skills, we needed a magnifying glass to read the little number.

I'm in the market for a 357. And I'm talking battery, not gun. I think that's the number anyway.

I only need one. Of course you can't buy just one of these little batteries. They're sold in pairs. Sure, maybe I'll save another 15 cents, but by the time I actually need the second battery, it won't be good anymore. I grab it and go.

There's other stuff on my list, but that's more than enough for today. I just want to pay and get out of here.

But not yet. I have one more choice to make.

Which checkout line do I stand in? There are three people in the Express line. Number 7 only has one person, but she has a full cart.

I stand there for a few seconds pondering my options and then see the guy from the toothpaste aisle.

"Left or right?" I ask him.

"Huh?"

"Pick one."

"Left."

And that's the direction I go.

■ ■ ■

The author's favorite tooth floss? Waxed, cinnamon flavor. Antiperspirant? Fresh scent. Everything else? Whatever's cheapest.

FENG SHUI AND THE PUBLIC RESTROOM

Like most guys, I don't have the eye, or the patience, for interior design. I can only take so much of it before wanting to scream. As far as I'm concerned, a beanbag chair is a fine piece of furniture. Better yet, I'm just as happy lying on the floor.

While I may not know good interior design when I see it, I do know when something isn't quite right. Case in point. Public restrooms. Who designs them?

Let's begin with the door itself. When it opens, you typically get a good look at guys doing what they went there to do. Personally, I like some privacy when I'm taking care of business. No, you can't see anything, but I'd rather not turn my head and see people strolling by. "Hello there, how ya doin? Sorry, I can't wave right now."

Next we have the automatic flushers, soap dispensers, faucets, hand dryers, and paper towel machines. Believe it or not, despite my limited knowledge of most things mechanical, I know how to operate the "old fashioned" manual variety of every one of these devices. I know how to turn them on, get just the right amount of stuff I need, whether it be soap or water or paper towels, and even how to shut them off. In fact, I've known this for quite some time.

The automatic ones don't operate the way I want them to. The commode flushes before I'm done and that leads to a fun game of "let's fool the little red light so it flushes again." One benefit is the additional exercise I get, standing up and down several times until I hear that magical flushing sound.

The automatic soap dispensers are ok, but the faucets never give you enough water. And that means it's time to play tricks on the red light again. Back and forth, back and forth with your hands until you've been given the proper ration of water. And of course, there are the dispensers with attitudes. The ones which don't give you any soap or water because they're having a bad day. Whatever.

I've never been a hand dryer kind of guy. I know they save trees and all, and are supposedly cleaner than paper towels, but give me the paper towels anyway. I can't get my hands dry enough with the dryer and have to keep turning that sucker on for another blast of Sahara Desert heat.

I must point out a design feature that I am strongly in favor of, one that you find in more and more casual restaurants these days. Plastered on the wall above the urinals at eye level is one of two things, today's sports page or some hot chick. Since I like to read while in the bathroom, the hands-free sports page is great. Most women, including my wife, just don't understand the appeal of reading the paper while answering nature's call. They have more of the "do what you have to and get out" mentality. Well, reading is part of my routine. And as for the hot chicks staring back at me, that's always a good thing, no matter where I am.

I just realized something. If I'm looking at pictures of hot chicks, what's in the ladies room? Photos of male models with their six-pack abs and beefy biceps? That's disgusting. My wife doesn't need to see that stuff.

COME AND GET IT!

I took some Tootsie Rolls to work recently. A super duper big bag we'd had for some time. So long in fact they'd gotten buried behind other stuff in our pantry and we'd forgotten about them. I found it while looking for something else.

"We still have those?" my wife asked when I set the bag on the counter. "I'll bet they're no good anymore."

I tried one. It was delicious, but I knew if we hadn't downed them by now, we weren't going to. We needed help. We needed .... the professionals. And they would be .... my coworkers. They'll eat anything. And lots of it.

I took the bag to work Monday morning. When I came in on Tuesday, they were gone, bag and all.

I knew they wouldn't let me down.

My coworkers are like vacuum cleaners. Scatter some free food around the office and they'll suck it up in no time.

And it doesn't matter what it is. Cookies, candy, doughnuts, asparagus. Set it out there, and like a magnet, they're attracted. Before you know it, bam!, it's gone.

"I don't like these," my wife said the other night as she pointed to the "intense" dark chocolate squares I'd bought her a while back. "They taste like wax."

That sounded appetizing.

I'm not a fan of dark chocolate, or wax, but I know who is.

They were gone before lunch.

I don't know if anyone liked them, but they didn't go to waste, and that was the important thing. I was glad they were gone, but I must admit, I was feeling a bit guilty. I probably should've warned them about the waxy taste.

Nah. Why spoil a good thing?

My wife made some potato soup recently. When I saw what all was in it, I declined. As it turns out, she wasn't all that wild about it either. She ate some but couldn't finish it. It's in the refrigerator just waiting to be disposed of.

Hmmm.

I bet a few plastic bowls and spoons in the office would take care of that.

NA NA NA NA NA NA!

They're in my mail box everyday. From my bank. My credit card company. Even my mother-in-law.

What are they? The annual privacy notice. That's a great name for something they don't keep private. They share my social security number and financial information with other companies and then said me a piece of paper telling me about it.

I normally look at these things for an average of 2 ¼ seconds before tossing them in the trash. But not this year. This year, I decided to take a closer look.

I'm not sure it was such a good idea.

This is what one of them said.

Do we share your personal information for our everyday business purposes? Heck yeah!

Can you do anything about it? Ha ha ha. That's a good one. You know what you can do about it? Not a d#$@ thing. Na na na na na na.

Do we share your personal information for our marketing purposes? You betcha.

Can you do anything about it? Yeah right.

Do we share your personal information for joint marketing with other companies? Cha ching! Yessir, and they pay us big bucks for it. You know those catalogs you've been getting from Eskimos R Us and Turkish Time Shares? That's why. We made a ton of money selling your personal information to them, as well as a bunch of other companies you've never heard of. Do you like kumquats? You're gonna get a special offer from Chinese Kumquats any day now.

Can you do anything about it? You sure can. Buy some of those kumquats and before you know it, you'll be getting even more crap from even more companies.

Do we share your personal information with people who don't like you? Of course we do. Why do you think your mother-in-law has been sending you stuff?

Can you do anything about it? Not really, although a restraining order against her might not be a bad idea.

If you would like to opt out of our joint marketing, call 1-888-kumquat and leave a message. No one listens to them, but it might make you feel a little better.

I put down the notice and picked up the phone.

"I want to cancel my credit card."

"I'm sorry to hear that Mr. Engle. Is there anything we can do to change your mind?"

"Ha ha ha. That's a good one."

"Are you sure? If you like, we'll send you more convenience checks at a rate of only 57% interest. We'll even reduce your annual interest rate from 38 ¾% to 38 ½%. You just name it. What can we do to keep your business?"

I thought about it for 2 ¼ seconds.

"Not a d#$@ thing! Na na na na na na."

EMSL - ENGLISH AS MY SECOND LANGUAGE

A brother-in-law of mine recently taught an English as a Second Language class to native Chinese speakers. The students could already speak English. The class focused more on conversational English and slang.

I should've signed up for his class.

Some of the things I hear people say anymore don't mean much to me, even though they're supposedly communicating in my native tongue.

"Selfie" had been around awhile before I'd even heard of it, let alone know what it was.

"A what?" I asked the first time I heard someone say it.

"It's when you take a picture of yourself."

"Ohhhhhhhhhhhhh".

When I was growing up, if you really liked something, it was neat, or cool, or even far out. Today, it's sick. Or dope. Or who knows what else.

But, if you're not feeling well, you know, you're really sick, what do you say then?

We like to shorten things too.

Instead of "all day, every day", it's 24/7/365.

A few years ago, I heard someone on TV use the expression "romcom".

I was confused.

And then, in a moment of unusual clarity and heightened awareness, I realized what it was.

She was referring to a particular type of move, a Romantic Comedy. A chick flick. You know, the kind of movie real guys aren't supposed to like, or even admit to watching?

"Nipslip". I just heard this one recently. Being a heterosexual male, I should've figured it out on my own but had to look it up.

And when I did, I just shook my head.

A "Nipslip" is a nipple slip, as in a specific type of Wardrobe Malfunction. You know, when your clothes malfunction. Like when they're not supposed to fall off but they do and a lot of people see it. Yeah, that happens to me all the time.

I often tune in to the business channel CNBC during lunch. The experts talk about things like "natgas" and "capX".

Natgas is Natural Gas. Not the kind I have, but the stuff you heat your home with.

CapX? Those are Capital Expenditures. That's when a company spends money on big things like buildings and equipment. Like if you or I buy a house or a new refrigerator.

I love baseball but even that's confusing sometimes. I couldn't tell you what all the new statistics mean or even some of the descriptions the announcers use. One guy talks about "taters", although he's not referring to the kind you eat. No, that's his word for when a batter "goes yard", as in, hits a home run.

Whatever.

Me and the woman were shootin' the breeze the other day. Talkin' about gettin' some new capX for our pad, but decided to wait a bit since we were a little light on dough.

I grabbed the Sports section and headed for the can. Had some nasty natgas.

She turned on the tube. Was watchin' a romcom and texting her bestie.

We went to that new place later for ribs. The food was sick.

We came home and did the nasty.

You got that?

Me neither.

THE ANNOUNCEMENT

I was reading the Sunday paper recently when I came across the engagement and wedding announcements. After glancing at a few of them, I saw a pattern that went something like this:

Mr. and Mrs. James Snobbynose, IV are thrilled to announce the recent engagement of their beautiful and intelligent daughter Allyson, to equally handsome and smart Biff Wallington, seventh son of renowned physician William and his charming wife Winnie.

Allyson attended prep school in Connecticut and graduated first in her class from Yale. She earned a Masters in Saving the Planet from Dartmouth and is now President and CEO of OneWorld-OneChoice, a nonprofit she began two years ago.

Biff graduated from Cal-Poly in only two and a half years and is the inventor of Postage PC, a fully functional laptop computer no larger than a first class stamp.

Allyson and Biff plan to wed this September outside of a quaint little country church in the Shenandoah Valley one hour before sunset. In addition to family, only their most important and attractive friends will be on hand to celebrate this blessed event. The couple will then leave immediately for a three month honeymoon to Bora Bora.

After the nausea had passed, I did the only thing I could to feel better about myself. I wrote one. What do you think?

Scooter Williams and his old lady are tickled pink to tell you their daughter Gladys, the ugly one, who they thought they'd never get rid of, has found a way to get herself engaged to some poor sucker named Bo. Bo has parents, we just don't really like them all that much and don't want to give them the satisfaction of seeing their name in the paper. They probably couldn't read it anyway.

Gladys decided she'd had enough school after ten years and is currently debating the merits of a GED. She doesn't see the point of having a job and likes to spend her days watching soaps. Luckily, Bo is a real go getter. He's the best dang hunter you've ever seen and earns his keep selling animal pelts. In his spare time, he grows tobacco in a secret location and makes a particularly strong brand of alcohol in his basement.

The couple hasn't pinned down a wedding date yet, but it will definitely be sometime in the next four months before the baby arrives. For their honeymoon, they'll stop at their favorite 7-Eleven for hot dogs and cherry Slurpees® before heading south to spend an afternoon at Luray Caverns.

My wife and I may not have gone to Bora Bora on our honeymoon, but I did take her to KFC and the Dairy Queen. Oh yeah, and we went bowling afterwards.

ONE OF THOSE DAYS

Wednesday
It's 5:20 in the morning and I'm trudging around the house, knee deep in snow, shining the flashlight to mark my way. What's wrong with this picture? Everything. I'm supposed to be driving to work right now, but that's not possible. Why? Because I can't find my car keys. And where do I think they are? Out here somewhere. In the two feet of snow surrounding my house. Wonderful.

Let's rewind.

Fifteen minutes ago
I go downstairs to leave. I realize I won't get far without car keys. I walk upstairs to the bedroom. To my surprise, they're not in the dresser drawer where I always keep them.

Fourteen minutes ago
Back downstairs. I check the coat I had on yesterday afternoon. I'm sure that's where they are. Wrong! Ok, now I'm confused, and a bit concerned. We're talking car keys, house keys, Post Office box key, a key to my dad's house and a few others that are for something, although for the life of me I couldn't tell you what. Did

I set them down somewhere in the basement? Maybe the laundry room? No. By the door? No. In my shoes? No.

And then it hits me. I know where they are.

Twelve minutes ago

Back upstairs. They're in the bedroom closet on top of my sweat pants. The same place I always leave my glasses when I can't find them. Wrong again. Now I'm more confused, and starting to panic. This isn't like me. My wife, maybe, but not me. I'm also getting agitated. I'm going to be late for work.

Ten minutes ago

Back to the basement. I know what I need to do, although I don't really want to do it. Yesterday afternoon, after I got home from work, I was knocking icicles off the gutters. I'll bet my keys fell out of my coat pocket somehow. Great. My wife tells me to take hers and look for mine when I get home from work. I can't do that. It would bug me all day. She turns on all the lights, inside and out to help me see. I pull my ski pants over my clothes. I need a flashlight. It's upstairs. I'm downstairs. My day isn't going well. After retrieving it, I put on my boots and out the door I go into the darkness. I retrace my steps, sinking into the snow just like I did the day before. When I complete my lap around the house, the only thing I have now are wet socks but no keys. I hate wet socks.

5:30

Back inside. I'm running out of places to look. Out of desperation, I reach into the outside pocket of my wife's purse. Guess what I find? Hmmmm. How'd they get there? I know I didn't put them there. Why would I? That only leaves one other person, and she's denying it. Apparently, it's going to remain an unsolved mystery.

I change my wet socks, take a few deep breaths to calm the nerves, and off to work I go. Halfway there, my stomach starts to growl. I've already worked off my breakfast. I'll eat something as soon as I get to the office.

No I won't.

I forgot to grab my lunch.

It's in the refrigerator.

It's going to be .... one of those days.

SAMOAS®, SHORTBREADS AND SAVANNAH SMILES®

A couple months ago, I ordered Girl Scout cookies from two co-workers. Three boxes from one and two from the other. Their girls were selling them for the first time. And my coworkers? I'd soon find out they were rookies as well.

When my first order arrived, so did an email.

"They're at my desk," she said. "Come and get'm!"

If the Post Office won't deliver on Saturday, I guess Girl Scout moms can do the same thing during the week.

When I got home, I was sure there'd been a mistake.

I opened one box and half the cookies were missing! Did she eat them?

And the ones that were there? They were roughly the size of a marble! My Savannah Smiles® didn't make me all that happy.

Ok, what's going on here? I paid four bucks a box. Where are my cookies?

A few days later, I got another email. This was for order #2.

"They're in the trunk of my car," he tells me. "Next time you go outside, let me know and we'll make the exchange."

The exchange? What is this? A drug deal? Obviously, Girl Scout dad isn't big on delivery either.

"What did you order?" he asked. I don't have the list."

"I don't know. We did this two months ago."

What kind of operation are we running here? This guy is an embarrassment to Girl Scout nation. He tried to blame it on his wife, saying she lost the order form.

At this point, I'm surprised they didn't give me a list of ingredients along with baking instructions and tell me to figure it out myself.

Yeah, I know, I shouldn't complain. This is for a good cause. But why should I have to suffer?

When I was a Girl Scout, I didn't treat my customers like this.

Ok, I never was a Girl Scout.

They didn't want me.

In years past, I wanted Girl Scout cookies more often than just this time of year. I'm not so sure about that now.

The next time, if there is one, this is what I want.

I want a *full* bag of cookies. "Man sized" cookies.

I want them delivered. To me. Not in someone's trunk.

And I want them for less than four bucks.

And if I don't get what I want?

I don't know. I haven't thought that far ahead.

Obviously, I was never a Boy Scout either.

■ ■ ■

Their website says to get your cookies directly from the Cookie Professional, the Girl Scout, not the parents. I wonder why.

ONE B.S. AND A LOT OF DOO-DOO

When I was in college, I earned a Bachelor of Science degree in Psychology. A B.S.

Why Psychology?

Because I found it interesting.

What was I going to do with a degree in Psychology?

I didn't have a clue.

As it turned out, I never did use it.

Despite all the different companies I worked for during my career, and all the different jobs I had, none of them required a Psychology background.

My brother-in-law majored in Chemistry. He went to work for a large oil company as a Chemist.

He was more focused and practical than I was in terms of what direction he wanted to go.

He raised his daughter to be the same way.

She got her degree in Computer Science and now works for a tech company.

He would never say it, but I'll bet he thinks my B.S. in Psychology is a bunch of BS.

I was reading a story the other day about a woman who's pursuing her doctorate degree and won a $20,000 award for her research.

I was impressed.

Until I read further.

She is editing and digitizing an almost 500 year old Latin manuscript that's based on a thirteenth century Old French veterinary manual.

Huh?

I kept reading.

She's "analyzing the symbiotic relationship between women and horses in medieval texts."

Say what?

She's "analyzing the symbiotic relationship between women and horses in medieval texts."

It didn't sound any better the second time.

Why on earth, or any place in the universe, would anyone want to do that?

Her goal is "to elucidate elements of interspecies communication, its effect on human linguistic and emotional growth, and its relation to the performance of gender and establishment of identity."

Wow. That's a mouthful.

I don't know much about horses, but I do know this.

That's the biggest pile of horse doo-doo I've ever heard.

And she won 20 grand for it?

What were the other applicants studying?

If my niece had told her dad that's what she wanted to study, or something like it, I can only imagine what he would've said.

Actually, I don't have to imagine what he would've said.

I know what he would've said.

"I don't think so."

Or maybe "Try again."
Or "Wrong answer."
Why?
Because he'd think it's a big pile of horse doo-doo.
And that ain't no BS.

■ ■ ■

The author likes horses but he doesn't like horse doo-doo. Or step-ping in it.

WHAT I MEANT TO SAY

My boss enters the crowded room and walks toward the microphone.

"Thanks for coming out folks. I appreciate you being here on such short notice. Let's get right to it. I'd like to introduce someone you all know very well. Our humor columnist Kevin Engle."

Raucous applause greets me as I stand and shake his hand.

"Thanks Dan. And thank you all very much. I'm grateful for the warm welcome. Please sit down."

I take a drink of water as the audience settles into their seats.

"Ladies and gentlemen, there's no easy way to say this and so I'll just say it. I'm stepping down immediately as the humor columnist for the newspaper."

A loud groan goes up from the crowd.

"I've given this a lot of thought. I need to spend more time with my family."

"Excuse me Mr. Engle," a reporter calls out, "but isn't it just you and your wife? And don't you see each other every day?"

"Yes, that's true. My wife and I do spend a lot of time together. What I meant to say is I need to take care of a few health concerns I've been neglecting for some time."

"But didn't your doctor just give you a clean bill of health?"

"Yes, he did. All my tests came back normal and I'm happy to report I'm in excellent shape. What I meant to say is I want to slow down a bit. Do some things I've been wanting to do. Play more golf. Go fly fishing."

"But don't you suck at golf? And don't you hate to fish?"

"Yeah, you're right, but I like to eat fish. What I meant to say is my wife and I want to travel and there are lots of places we want to see."

"Is that really a good idea right now with all the news about possible terrorist attacks on commercial airliners?"

"Probably not. My wife and I are both a little skittish about flying. What I meant to say is I've been doing this for almost three years now and I'm a bit burned out. I'm just not enjoying it as much as I used to.

"But weren't you quoted in a recent interview that this column is the best thing you've done in quite some time?"

"I did say that. I really do like it, especially when I get feedback from my readers. What I meant to say is Dan and I have talked about this and we've decided to part ways. It's time the paper went in a different direction."

"You got canned didn't you?"

"I did, but I got a really nice severance package."

"Is there a Kevin Engle in here?" a voice calls out from the back of the room. "I got your pizza."

"Excuse me everyone. My severance package just arrived."

TIMING BELTS AND TORQUE CONVERTERS

"Mr. Engle?"

"Yeah, what's up?" I said as the name of the garage appeared on the caller ID. "Is my car ready to go?"

"Not quite. It will pass inspection, but we found some things you might want to consider having done."

I hate these conversations. Phone calls from the garage fall into two categories. Either my car is fine and ready to go, or my car will be fine, after I pay a gazillion dollars to fix things I never even knew it had.

Clearly, this call was headed toward the latter category, the one that was about to cost me a lot of money.

I'm not much of a car guy. My interest in and knowledge of vehicles and internal combustion engines goes as far as putting gas in the tank and paying my yearly AAA dues.

What I heard next sounded something like this.

"Blah, blah, blah, two million dollars. Do you play the lottery?" he asked and then laughed.

I didn't care for his humor. I swallowed hard and begin thinking of my soon-to-be non-existent checking account balance.

He continued, talking of the importance of torque converters, solenoids and crankshaft flywheels, all things that made me think of *Star Wars, Episode 3*. "Oh yeah, and the timing belt is starting to show some cracks too. That could go at any time."

Finally, something I understood. "And that's why my clock has been running slow right?"

"Huh?" he replied, as if I'd just said something incredibly stupid.

When you don't know much about vehicles, you have to trust the person telling you what's wrong with yours. I'm not the most trusting person in the world, especially when someone is trying to persuade me to give them money.

"So would you like us to take care of these things?"

Now I repeated his line. "Huh?" My head was swimming in a sea of solenoids and crankshafts.

"Do you want us to do the work?"

"Not today. I have to check my lottery numbers first."

Now he was the one who wasn't laughing.

"Ok," he said in that tone that's supposed to make you feel foolish for not doing what he suggested, "but I wouldn't wait too long."

A few days later, I overheard a group of female coworkers talking about car troubles.

"He said I need a new timing belt."

Being the helpful person I am, I had to chime in.

"I'll bet you're having problems with your car's clock aren't you?"

"Huh," she said as she looked at me and wrinkled up her face in confusion, as if I'd just said something incredibly stupid.

"Ah, nothing."

She obviously wasn't interested in expanding her limited knowledge of vehicles.

I tried.

3 K'S, 2 C'S AND NO H

My dad had a hard time remembering people's names. I'm the same way.

I used to work with a guy who has three kids. Two sons and a daughter. I could never remember their names. And he knew it.

Instead of asking him every time, and feeling totally stupid, I'd have to do it in that roundabout way and hope he'd play along.

"How's your oldest son?" or, "What's going on with your daughter?"

"Chris is applying to graduate school," he'd say, telling me his name for the 400th time. "Madison loves first grade. And she talks all the time."

"And your son in college?"

"Ryan's doing well. Hardly working, but getting good grades."

Five minutes later, I'd forgotten them again.

And then there's Kathy. I know five of them. Make that three. The other two spell their name with a C. Three K's and two C's. Do you think I can keep track of who's a K and who's a C?

I can't.

Every time I send them an email, or write their name, I'm never sure it's right and have to double check. Sorry Kathy. And Cathy.

Would they be upset if I got it wrong?

Maybe. Maybe not. I should ask them.

No one has spelled Kevin with a C, but they do mess up my last name and that bothers me.

Every year, at Christmas, we receive a few cards where our last name is misspelled. My wife says it's no big deal. I guess she's right, but yet, it gets under my skin.

We've known these folks for years.

By now, they should know how to spell our name. At least I think they should.

One year, after getting their card, I sent them an email gently reminding them it's E-n-g-l-e.

It didn't work.

They got it wrong the next year, and every year since.

Maybe they have a mental block, like I seem to with my co-worker's kids, and with Kathy and Cathy.

My best friend in school was Jon. That's right. No H. I wonder if he ever wished his parents would've just thrown it in to make his life easier? And to top it off, people always misspelled and mispronounced his last name too.

I guess I shouldn't complain, but I've been fighting these battles ever since I was little.

People called me Keith when I was a kid. I didn't like it. I despised that name.

Maybe that's why I'm overly sensitive about the subject now.

Then again, with my personality, I should just be glad people even talk to me, no matter what they call me.

So go for it.

Spell Kevin with a C if you want. Or two E's. And who cares if you mess up my last name.

And keep sending those Christmas cards.

Just don't call me Keith.

Please.

IT'S A HOUSE, NOT A CABIN!

When I was a little boy, people often called me the wrong name. Instead of Kevin, I got Keith. Nothing against Keith, but that wasn't my name. Oh by the way, my mother said I was going to be Kimberly if I had been a girl. I guess my parents liked the letter K. Anyway, I got tired of answering to Keith. You can only correct people so many times before giving up. And then, you're stuck with it.

Which brings me to my point.

My wife and I recently moved into a new home. A log home. Believe it or not, it took more than twenty years for this to become a reality. Our builder was slow, yes, but not that slow. Whenever I tell people we live in a log house, the response is usually something like "I love log cabins!" I don't want to be too picky, but it's not a cabin. Thus, in defense of my name and my home, and what the heck, my honor as well, I'd like to clear up some common misconceptions about log houses. Here goes.

- it's a house, not a cabin. When people tell me they love log cabins, I'd like to point out that Log Cabin® is syrup and

I love that too, especially on pancakes. When I think of a cabin, I imagine a small, dark, one room building. Our house has several rooms and even a garage. And we have lights too.

- we don't have an outhouse, although I could go to the bathroom outside if I really wanted to. Most of the time, I don't, choosing instead to use the indoor facilities, particularly in the colder months. Frostbite can be a nasty thing, especially on certain parts of the body.

- we opted not to go with dirt floors. Too messy. Instead, we upgraded to carpet and wood, definitely more expensive than dirt. One selling point of dirt is the low upkeep. We'll keep that in mind next time.

- we don't have to wear animal furs to stay warm, although we do wear clothes, most of the time. Wood is a natural insulator. If constructed properly, a log house is just as energy efficient and warm, if not more so, as a "conventional" home.

- people who live in log homes aren't necessarily hunters. Yeah, my wife is, but she doesn't shoot all of our food. I actually go to the grocery store and buy our rations. I am having trouble finding one that trades in pelts though.

- it even looks nice. Yeah, it does. Our goal wasn't to build an ugly home, especially after waiting for it for so long.

- this is not a second home. It is not our retirement home. This is our "365 days a year" home. Some folks actually choose to live in a log home year round. Ok, it was my wife's idea.

I was feeling pretty good about this log home public service announcement until I recently overheard two acquaintances talking. The conversation went something like this.

"Did you hear Keith lives in a log cabin?"

"Really? I love log cabins!"

I give up.

GROCERY GRIPES

My wife hates to grocery shop. If it were up to her, we wouldn't eat very often. But since I've gotten into the habit of three meals a day, guess who goes to the store each week? I don't mind, although there are some things about it that I could do without.

For instance, my first encounter is with abandoned shopping carts loitering in the parking lot, just waiting to cause trouble. Don't you think they'd rather hang out with their friends in the cart return before working their next shift? I'd rather they did, as opposed to lurking next to my car door, ready to inflict paint damage on a moment's notice.

Once inside, I can only shake my head in frustration over what people do with their shopping carts. Ever turn the corner into the next aisle and come cart to cart with an orphaned metal food carrier? It sits there patiently, in the middle of the aisle of course, full of food, just waiting for its current owner to return from some far off journey. Ok, I've forgotten to grab the grapes and had to go back to get them from time to time, but I don't leave my cart sitting in the middle of traffic. Would you do that with your automobile? Don't answer that.

Don't you love it when you come across people who act like they're the only ones in the store? They stand there, in the middle of the aisle, deep in thought, as they study every variety of Campbell's® soup, snarling traffic in all directions. Wake up!

Ever see someone pick up an apple and a whole bushel of them comes tumbling to the floor? Did they look both ways and then walk off as if nothing happened? If so, you can be sure you've just identified a shopping cart deserter as well. Alert the food police!

Once you've successfully navigated your way through the food aisles, now it's time to do the same in the checkout line. Just be careful not to get behind the mathematically-challenged shoppers. They're the ones who don't think anyone will notice they have 25 items, yet they're standing in the 15 item express line. Or how about getting stuck behind the person who rushes off to scoop up a gallon of ice cream when he should be paying for his food? Or hearing those dreaded words that every shopper hates: "Price check on aisle 2!" And the self-checkout scanners that never seem to work right? Yeah, that's fun.

And what's the deal with coupons and shopping cards? Why can't the store just give me the sales price? Why do I have to fumble around with these miniscule scraps of paper, as well as those plastic cards that compete for space in my already-overcrowded wallet or keychain? If you want to put something on sale, why make me work for it? Isn't it enough that I'm already shopping in your store?

Let's not forget those people who like to invade your personal space in the checkout line. Can I please have enough room to put my groceries on the belt and sign my charge card receipt without getting claustrophobic?

Finally, what about those plastic bags that seem to be magnetically attracted to each other? You couldn't open them if your life depended on it, which it often does because the shoppers behind you are breathing down your neck, pressuring you to pick up the pace. Hey, I didn't come here to see how fast I could bag my stuff. Back off buddy!

Maybe it's time I took my medicine and asked my wife to do the grocery shopping from now on. Yeah, I'll bet she'd be up for that.

DRESS CODE

It was dinner time and we were tired and hungry. We'd hiked more than ten miles. Ten tough miles. Lunch had been our typical hiker's lunch of granola bars, trail mix and Gatorade. I wanted something a little more substantial for supper.

We stopped at one of the National Park lodge restaurants on the drive back to our cabin.

We hadn't been here before.

"Should we eat in or carry out?" my cousin asked.

From the way he said it, I sensed he wanted to do take out since we hadn't showered yet.

Me, I was more concerned about my stomach than my appearance. I wanted to eat. Now. Plus, all the restaurants in the Park were pretty laid back and didn't really care what you looked like.

"Let's check it out first and then decide."

We walked in the door and the hostess blocked our path, heading us off before we could go another step.

"May I help you?" she asked, defending all that was behind her.

I spotted what I thought was the menu hanging on the wall in front of us but asked to see one anyway.

Without giving us one, she said, "We have a 'bit of a dress code'. Shirts with collars for the guys, and a jacket."

My untucked hiking shirt had a collar. So did my cousin's. And my rain coat was in the trunk, although I didn't think that was the kind of jacket she was referring to.

My wife and I were wearing ball caps and all of us had on hiking shoes and pants.

It was obvious we didn't quite measure up to the dress code.

"Dinner is a five course meal," she went on, as if trying to discourage us even more. "Eighty-eight dollars."

"Oh."

Everyone standing there, including another employee who was doing her best to avoid eye contact with us, as well as not laugh, knew we wouldn't be eating there even if it was free.

"We also serve breakfast," the hostess continued, steering the conversation away from dinner. "And lunch is a bit more casual."

At that moment, I didn't care about breakfast or lunch, although I have to give her credit. She was polite and doing all she could to get rid of us without saying so. I got the impression she'd done this before.

"Obviously we're not dressed for dinner. We've been hiking all day," I explained, as if she couldn't figure that out on her own.

"There's a good pizza place down the road," she said. "They have an outdoor deck."

So much for subtlety.

Surely we were presentable enough to sit outside and eat.

We said thanks and headed for the car.

An older couple passed us along the way. He had on a jacket and tie. His wife, a dress. They obviously got the memo. The look they gave us was priceless.

Once back in the car, we sat there for several minutes and laughed.

We started for the pizza place but turned around shortly before getting there. I remembered it was just outside the National Park and our weekly Pass had expired the day before. Eat pizza on the deck and we'd have to pay another 25 bucks just to get back in the Park.

We were hungry, but not that hungry.

There was still trail mix to finish.

■ ■ ■

The author can now proudly say he was asked to leave a restaurant. He's such a badass.

THE PROFESSOR AND THE POTTER

I go to the eye doctor every year. And lately, every year, he tells me I need new glasses. This year his daughter broke the news. She's an eye doctor too.

It seems I'm at that age, somewhere between "getting older" and dead, where my eyes don't do what they used to. Tell me about it.

So I'm looking for new frames. I like the ones I already have. Why not get something similar?

"Oh no!" my wife says. "You can't do that! You've got to change! Mix it up! Do something different!"

Really? Why?

"I like you," I tell her. "I love you. Am I supposed to trade you in every few years just to make a change?"

It was a rhetorical question.

She didn't care for it.

But I had a point. If you really like something, do you have to change, just to change?

Apparently, she wasn't the only one who thought so.

There was that new eye doctor. She picked out frames that were "stylish".

Sure, if I want to look like I just got off the racquetball court, ok, yeah, they're stylish.

"And their rimless," she tells me. "That's in."

"Whoa, rimless! I gotta have those!" I said sarcastically.

She liked them. My wife liked them. The eye doctor's wife liked them. And one of their relatives did too.

Four females against me.

And my good friend, the male eye doctor? What did he have to say?

Nothing. He mumbled something about knowing when to keep your mouth shut.

Unfortunately, I never learned to do that.

And besides, I'm a man, full of testosterone and facial hair. I wasn't about to be pushed around by four females.

"Hey, they're *my* glasses," I told them. I'm the one who's wearing them."

"Yeah," the eye doctor's wife said. "But we have to look at you."

Ouch!

"How about these?" I asked as I tried another pair on.

With every frame I chose, their sneers said it all. No matter what I picked, they favored the "stylish" ones.

And then, I found them. They reminded me of a certain doctor. Dr. Jones, the archeology professor. Yeah, that guy. Indiana Jones. They were round and studious looking. They were perfect. The ladies rolled their eyes.

A week later, my new glasses showed up in the mail, along with the stylish ones. They wanted me to compare them one more time. Make sure that's what I really wanted.

I'd already made my choice.

And now, when I look in the mirror, I hear that music from the movie. I get the urge to travel to distant lands, battle the bad guys and find the treasure.

And it's all because of my new glasses.

The next day, a coworker noticed immediately. "Hey, you got new specs."

"That's right," I said proudly as the music started to play in my head.

"You look like Harry Potter."

Oh geez!

■ ■ ■

Harry Potter did save the world. Ok, so I look like Harry Potter.

WHAT'S A GUY TO DO?

Saturday evening.

My wife and I are visiting good friends at their house.

They've recently had a baby. Their first.

We're talking, laughing, being goofy, just like always.

And then, without warning, I see it.

I look over at mom and she's breast feeding. Right in front of us.

She's covered up. Sort of. But not totally.

My face gets hot.

I start to sweat.

I'm not supposed to be seeing this.

I pull a muscle in my neck as I quickly look away.

I don't glance over again until I'm sure the coast is clear.

"Oh my," I say to my wife on the ride home.

"Yup."

"I wasn't expecting that."

"Nope."

That incident occurred more than 20 years ago.

It happened again last month. Same situation, different people.

Now we're spending the weekend with my family, including a new addition.

It's a gorgeous Saturday and we're tailgating before a college football game. Between bites of my sausage sandwich, I look at my wife, and on the ground, in front of her, is my nephew's wife, breast feeding her baby boy.

She too is covered up. But not totally.

I almost jumped up out of my chair.

And just like the last time, I snapped my neck to the right, again pulling that same muscle.

"Move away from the area!" my inner voice screamed.

"Get more chips!"

"Go to the porta potty!"

"Just go somewhere else!"

"Oh my," I said to my wife later that night when the subject came up.

"Yup."

"I wasn't expecting that."

"Nope."

Hey, I'm open-minded.

For the most part.

Ok, maybe not that much.

I know that breast feeding is natural, it's beautiful, it's a bond between mother and child, blah blah blah.

But I'm also old-fashioned. When mom is doing it right in front of me, I'm uncomfortable.

I squirm.

What's a guy to do in that situation?

You can't look at mom because she might think you're looking at, you know.

Should I take off my shirt and toss it her way, hoping she'll use it to cover up?

Or should I shut my eyes and take a two hour nap?

Or should I just take off running and screaming?

I should've said something. Made a joke about it. But I didn't.
And I don't want to upset anyone, but geez.
If it ever happens again, I know one thing for sure.
I'm gonna have a sore neck.

PRICELESS? PERHAPS. FREE? FAR FROM IT.

I'm proud of my wife. But if she keeps it up, we're going to need a government bailout.

She's part of a work team who recently won a prestigious Corporate Performance Award. You go girl!

As part of the award, she and her fellow team members each get an all expenses paid trip to San Antonio to be recognized. Very cool.

Even cooler? She's allowed to take a guest. I wasn't her first choice, but I'm going.

Free airfare. Free hotel. Free food.

I'm liking this. Like the MasterCard commercials, it's priceless. But free? Far from it.

First of all, the IRS doesn't know the meaning of the word. That free airfare, free hotel and free food? They all get added on to her income for the year. And that means taxes have to be paid.

The dinner/award ceremony is a formal affair.

Judy needs a new dress. Cha-Ching.

I need a new suit. Cha-Ching.

She needs a slip to wear under her dress. Cha-Ching.

My new suit needs to be altered. Cha-Ching.

She needs new shoes. Cha-Ching.

I need new shoes. Cha-Ching.

She needs a purse. Cha-Ching.

I need a new tie to match my suit. Cha-Ching.

Do you see a pattern here? I do and I don't like it.

The big event occurs only hours after we get off the plane, and that's why we're supposed to store all those new clothes in the overhead bin above our seat. If we checked our bags and they went elsewhere, we'd be out of luck.

That means we need a garment bag. I already have one. Excellent!

Not so fast. It's too big to fit in the overhead compartment.

Guess what I just bought? Cha-Ching.

Judy has a nice ring she'd like to wear, but it needs to be re-sized. Cha-Ching.

When we get there, she wants to have her hair done. Cha-Ching.

I have no hair. I always knew that would pay off some day.

And when we get home, there'll be airport parking. Cha-Ching.

Debt counseling. Cha-Ching.

And trips to the psychologist to learn how to handle all of this financial stress. Cha-Ching.

There's an important lesson here, and I'm going to share it with you. For free. It pays to be a slacker at work. Cha-Ching.

GOTTA GO!

I hear it's normal.

That's good to know.

I guess.

It started out every now and then, and before I knew it, turned in to a habit.

Ok, not a habit, but a necessity.

I'm sound asleep.

And then I'm not.

I wake up in the middle of the night.

Two seconds later, I know why.

I have to go to the bathroom.

But I don't want to go to the bathroom.

I'm warm, all snug in my bed.

I don't want to get up.

I'm lazy.

I don't want to take the 15 seconds to do what I need to.

No, I'd rather lie here for ten minutes, fighting with myself.

The conversation in my head, between Smart Me and Lazy Me, goes something like this.

"Just get up!"

"But I don't want to."

"You'll feel more comfortable."

"You're right. But I don't want to."

"Don't be stupid! You'll be done in no time."

"Yeah, I know, but I still don't want to."

This debate plays out almost every night.

If I'd just get up and go, I'd already be back in bed, falling asleep, with an empty bladder.

But no, I'm still lying here. Awake and uncomfortable.

Maybe I should wear a diaper to bed? Then I wouldn't have to get up. I could fall back asleep and empty the ol' bladder any time I wanted. It's the best of both worlds.

Oh boy.

I have seen the future and it is not good.

■ ■ ■

Something else the author isn't looking forward to is, uh, uh. He can't remember now.

Q & (NO) A

"Kevin Engle, I want to see **YOU** on Jeopardy!®"

"Did you hear that? He said my name! Alex Trebek said my name! On TV!"

"Huh?" my wife asked as she looked up from her knitting to see what I was babbling about.

"Thanks Alex! I'll be there!"

That's not really what Alex Trebek said, but I swear it's what I heard.

The host of the long running game show Jeopardy!® was encouraging his viewers to become contestants and the first step in that process was taking an online test.

I signed up the next day.

I like Jeopardy!®. My wife and I typically tune in each night.

"How do you know all this stuff?" she'll ask as I fire off the answers.

"I don't know. I just do."

Some people remember important stuff, like their wife's birthday and their kid's names. I remember Jeopardy!® stuff.

The online test would be my first step toward riches and fame. And at 7:00 Tuesday night, I would begin to make that happen.

I logged on and waited for the test to begin. There'd be 50 questions and I'd have 15 seconds for each.

"The test will start in 10 seconds. Nine, eight, seven, ..."

Here we go.

Question #1. Who was the Queen of France for less than three months in 1514?

Ahhhhh, ahhhhh.

Question #2. According to Greek mythology, what goddess was born an adult by emerging from her father's head and wearing armor?

Huh?

Question #3. This bird is a member of the Spheniscidae family and builds its nest with pebbles.

The cuckoo? I don't know.

Question #4. What singer, born in the West Indies, had a chart topping song in 2008?

Bruce Springsteen?

Wrongggggggggggggggggggggggg!!!

Question #5. What Canadian province is home to the city of Vancouver?

Finally, one I know! I've been there! It's, it's, Alberta!

Bzzzzzzzzzzzzzzzzzzzz!

British Columbia.

Question #6. Mark Harmon, the actor, stars in what popular TV show?

Ok, I got it! I've watched that show!

CSI! Right?

Almost, you loser. NCIS.

Dang!

And so it went. Twelve and a half minutes later, my Jeopardy!® hopes of fame and fortune were about as likely to come true as me becoming the next Queen of France and building a castle made of pebbles.

At 7:30, I tuned in to that night's show and watched as Alex quizzed the three contestants with tough questions like these.

What's the third letter of the alphabet?

Huh?

How many states are in the United States of America?

What?

What color is the sun?

You're kidding?

I went to bed that night, disappointed, dejected and depressed. My only hope was that other people had a hard time with the test as well. Or maybe I was the only one who took it. Yeah, that's it. Maybe no one else in the world other than me gave it a shot. It wouldn't matter how poorly I did, because I'd still have the best score. Yeah, I'll bet that happened.

Sorry Alex. I don't think I'll be seeing you anytime soon.

Hey, what about Wheel of Fortune®? I've always wanted to meet Vanna.

■ ■ ■

That Queen of France? Mary Tudor. The Greek goddess? Athena. And that bird? The penguin.

GOING, GOING, GONE

It's a pretty winter day. The snow is falling and I'm in my office, working at the computer and listening to classical music. It's one of those satellite radio stations you get through your TV.

And then I hear a crackling sound as the music starts to fade in and out.

I know what's coming next. I've been down this path before.

Instead of the song title and artist scrolling up and down my TV screen, I see something more ominous.

"Partial Signal Loss".

Going, going …

And then a few seconds later, "Complete Signal Loss".

Gone.

Thanks to the snow on my satellite dish, which is on the roof where I can't get to it, my TV reception is out.

The first time this happened a few years ago, I called the satellite company and asked what I could do.

"Can you spray off the snow with a garden hose?"

Did she really ask me that?

She did.

The answer to her question was no. I'd turned off the water and drained the line in November. And even if I did turn on the water, getting up on a ladder wasn't an option since what used to be my yard was now one big chunk of ice.

When the TV went out again the following winter, I decided it was time to get that satellite dish off the roof.

When spring came, I called the satellite company and the guy tried to but couldn't find a spot in the yard that would work for one reason or another.

I was stuck with it where it was.

Yeah, I could switch to cable but that sounded like too much hassle.

And so, here we go again.

Sometimes when it snows, I get all the channels. Other times, I get some. Today, I got none.

How am I supposed to survive without television? No satellite music. No sports. No soap operas.

How did people live before television?

I could read?

I already did that today.

How about hanging up those pictures we just had framed?

That's on the list for tomorrow.

My wife and I could play Go Fish, but she's out of town.

As a kid, I remember when all you needed to watch television, was a television.

You didn't need a connection to the cable company or a satellite dish on your roof.

When the guy was here last year to relocate the dish, he said I could spray it with cooking spray to prevent the snow and ice from sticking to it.

I should've listened to him.

Maybe I can watch something online instead? Something I wanted to see but missed. Or how about the news?

I found the broadcast.

Oh wait.

That was last night's news.

I've already seen last night's news.

Last night.

I want to see today's news.

Preferably, today.

I just had a scary thought.

The Super Bowl is this Sunday.

And guess what else is supposed to be here?

More snow.

If I miss the game, and the commercials, I won't be happy.

But wait, my wife gets home Friday. She's not afraid of heights.

I'll get out the hose and turn on the water.

And hold the ladder for her.

AN ACCIDENT WAITING TO HAPPEN

According to the picture on the back of the package of my shiny red Swiss Army knife, a gift from my brother-in-law and his wife, this thing has 15 different tools. At the moment, it could have 1500 and it wouldn't matter because I can't get the dang thing out of the hard plastic case. I need a Swiss Army knife to open my Swiss Army knife.

Ten minutes later, after my wife has come to the rescue, I still can't use it. Not until I open it, tool by tool, and that's easier said than done. I can already see this thing is an accident waiting to happen. Sharp pointy objects scare me. I appreciate the thoughtfulness, but I'm not so sure this was the best gift for me. I like having ten fingers.

Using the picture to guide me, I'm in search of 15 tools. Here goes.

Numbers one and two. Large blade and small blade? Check, check.

Three. A corkscrew? Check. That's for opening wine bottles right? I've never done that before. Does this mean I have to now?

Four and five. A can opener with a screwdriver? Check, check.

Six and seven. A bottle opener with a larger screwdriver? Check, check.

Eight. A wire stripper? Check. I've never stripped wires either. My mama told me not to play with fire or electricity. I always listened to what mama said.

Nine. A reamer? Check. What's a reamer?

Ten. A key ring? Check.

Eleven and twelve. Tweezers and a toothpick? I'm not sure yet. I can't find them. I'll come back to those.

Thirteen. Scissors? Check. I could've used those ten minutes ago.

Fourteen. A multi-purpose hook? I can see it, but I can't get it out. Ok, I got it, but now my fingernail is gone.

And fifteen. Wood saw? Check. Since my wife won't let me have a chain saw, for my own safety, I hope this is big enough to cut down that dead tree in our yard.

Breaking news! My wife found the tweezers and toothpick and freed them as well. I knew she could do it.

As I inspect my new 15 function accident-waiting-to-happen tool, I have a few questions.

Number one. Shouldn't you be in the Swiss Army to own one of their knives?

Number two. What's a reamer?

And lastly. My brother-in-law and his wife know I'm not your handyman, wine bottle opening, lumberjack, tool kind of guy. Didn't they realize I could hurt myself with this thing?

Hmmm.

And I always thought they liked me.

IT'S KEVIN. PLEASE.

"Ok Mr. Engle, you're good to go."

I was at the dealer having the oil changed and tires rotated on my wife's car. The same place I always go to for this stuff. And the same folks wait on me every time. Today it was Brad, as it usually is.

And that's what I call him. Brad. He calls me Mr. Engle.

"It's Kevin," I said.

He laughed. We've had this conversation before.

I get it. In business, you're supposed to treat your customers with respect. And that's fine, but I'd rather be called by my first name.

Don't call me Sir or Mister. It's Kevin. Please.

The first time someone called me 'Mr. Engle', I wasn't sure they were talking to me. It made me feel old.

Even to this day, when I hear it, I think of my dad, not me, and he's not around anymore.

Sure, I'm in my 50's. My early 50's. That's not old right? I don't think so.

It was when I was a kid, but now that I'm there, heck no.

For whatever reason, I still think of myself as a 20 or 30 something, although when the knees are sore and the back is stiff, maybe closer to forty.

To me, "old" is a state of mind, a moving target. If you haven't caught up to it yet, you're doing well.

My parents taught me to respect your elders. And that meant saying Mr. and Mrs. to adults.

Now that I'm on the other side of that greeting, I don't like it so much.

Growing up, I had great neighbors. Mr. and Mrs. James on one side. The Paxtons on the other. And the Cooks two doors down.

Today, the Paxtons live in Florida. Three years ago, my wife and I were passing through and stopped in to visit. It was the first we'd seen them in a long time.

They were just as friendly as ever, and looked like I remembered.

"Mr. and Mrs. Paxton, it's great to see you!"

"Hey, none of that Mr. and Mrs. crap!" he said with his usual sense of humor. "It's Ed and Eleanor."

And so that's what I called them, when I remembered to do so. But it was strange. No matter how old I am, they'll always be Mr. and Mrs. to me. That was their name.

Sorry Ed.

Old habits die hard.

And the next time I was at the dealer getting the car serviced? And Brad was helping me?

"Ok Mr. Engle, …"

I give up. You can't train these young kids today.

PLAIN ENGLISH

English is my native language. In fact, it's my *only* language. But more and more, I seem to understand it less and less.

The other day at work for instance, I read an email from my company's CEO that made me laugh. I don't think that's what she was trying for, but she did a good job. And I don't know her personally, but I'm fairly certain she's a native English speaker like me, although that wasn't clear from what I read. As far as I could tell, she wrote it in another language. Corporate-speak.

She discussed "sunsetting" the corporate brand, the "value proposition" and the "overarching brand story". Does that last one have something to do with McDonalds and the golden arches?

Do people really talk like this? And are we supposed to understand them? I'll bet their dinner conversations are fascinating.

She went on to mention "the breadth of our capabilities". I think what she was saying is that we can do a lot of different things.

Here's what else she said, and how I'd translate it into plain English.

"Cross-business collaboration"

We share stuff with our coworkers.

"Mission-critical"

Important.

"A leader in the space."

We're #1.

"A solid collective value proposition."

Ok, I give up. I don't have a clue about that one.

I'm ashamed to admit it, but even my wife is starting to sound like this. She throws around the abbreviations as if I'm supposed to know what they mean.

She talks about BG&O's, PMR's, telcons and flowdown.

BG&O's. Business goals and objectives. I thought the BG&O was one of the railroads in Monopoly?

PMRs. Program Management Reviews.

Telcon. To me, it sounds like a secret military operation. Not quite. How about a teleconference?

And flowdown? You know what they say runs down hill? I get a lot of flowdown at work.

When people speak English, I'd like to understand their English. Maybe I should invent a new device. I'll call it the Mumbo Jumbo 5000. Whenever someone starts spouting corporate-speak, the Mumbo Jumbo 5000 will magically decode and decipher what they really mean in words that I can understand.

I do know one thing. There's a high probability this written piece may have a detrimental impact on my future promotional possibilities within the organization who pays my wages. In addition, someone at a more senior level than me on the organizational chart, which is just about everyone, may tell me my current skill set and developmental path aren't congruent with the mission and vision of the company and that I'd be best suited applying those skills in a different setting.

In plain English, I'm gonna get canned!

■ ■ ■

In the world of humor writing, Engle's Angle is a leader in the space. And that's no flowdown!

THE KEY TO HAPPINESS

1:30 Saturday afternoon. Give or take.

My wife is gone and won't be back for an hour or two. I'm in the garage emptying the Shop-Vac®. I've been using it to suck up stink bugs. I dump the dead little beasts in the garbage and clean crud off the filter before reassembling it. I'll wash it out in the laundry tub as well.

I grab the door knob, turn and push. The door into the basement opens, but only about a quarter of an inch. I jiggle it back and forth several times and get the same result. Along with a sinking feeling in my gut.

I'm locked out. The cleaning people must have accidentally locked it this morning.

Of course I don't have a key. Why would I? I don't carry a house key unless I'm leaving the house. My cell phone? It's upstairs.

I stand there for a minute, considering my options, already knowing they're not good.

I can go outside, but it's January and I'm not dressed for it.

I could bust open the door, or try, but that doesn't sound so good. No doubt I'd hurt myself in the process and end up with a broken door, along with an angry wife. Scratch that.

I try picking the lock. Let's just say I wouldn't make a good crook.

I go outside and check the front door to confirm what I already know. I'd feel pretty stupid if I discovered later it was unlocked. Even more stupid than I feel right now.

And like a cold winter wind slapping me across the face, reality sets in. I'm trapped. In my garage.

Ok, I accept my situation. How can I make the best of it? Isn't that what you're supposed to do in times like these?

Since I'm in the garage, I could organize the garage, a chore I always put off for one reason or another. Just like I'm going to today.

I crush a few soda cans and drop them in the recycling bin, along with some cardboard. I root around in the old newspaper stack and find something to read. After several minutes of staring at two nearly identical photos trying to find the 12 differences between them, I give up. I only found one and I have more pressing things on my mind at the moment. Like a full bladder that's making it hard to focus on anything else. I could take care of that outside, in the woods, but with no leaves on the trees, my neighbors would have a front row seat. I'm a modest guy. I'll hold it. For now.

I open the door to my car and climb in. I recline the seat and shut my eyes. I haven't had my nap today. This seems like as good a time as any.

I hear the dishwasher running in the kitchen above me and the radio playing in the basement. I check the clock. My wife won't be here for at least another hour. I'd asked her to stop at the store and pick up some bandages. I hope she forgets. All I want right now is to see her red car in the driveway.

As I'm lying there, I think about what I can do to make sure this never happens again, like hiding a key outside. We've talked about it for years but haven't done it. That was smart. Another thought crosses my mind. What if Judy doesn't have her house keys with her? When we're out together, she doesn't always take them. Nah, she'll have them. I hope.

I nod off, but wake up every 10 or 15 minutes. My toes are getting cold and so am I. I'm thinking more seriously about a trip to the woods to care of some business.

I hear the phone ring and the voice of Caller ID.

"Virginia call."

I'd bet a pack of toe warmers that's her telling me she's on her way. Fifteen minutes later, I see her beautiful red car coming up the driveway. Thank God. I've been stuck here for an hour and 45 minutes. A great way to spend my Saturday afternoon.

"What are you doing?" she asks when she sees me get out of the car.

I tell her my predicament, including the part about my pressing matters.

"You have your house keys don't you?"

She hesitated, and I got that sinking feeling again.

"Here they are," she said as she pulled them out of her backpack.

I grabbed them and ran for the door.

■ ■ ■

On a cold Saturday afternoon, the author learned the true key to happiness was just that. A key.

BLAH, BLAH, BLAH

Sixteen days, three graduations. Two for family, one for friends. One road trip, a $5 bottle of water, two $6 soft pretzels, three cities, three states, six airports and nine Egg McMuffins® later, we survived. Bankrupt, but still breathing.

"Are you sure you want to do this?" my wife asked last year when I foolishly suggested it.

I should've listened to her. As usual.

The first two ceremonies lasted about an hour and 45 minutes each. Not bad. The last one? Three hours and 45 minutes! Yikes!

Three versions of Pomp and Circumstance. Three boring speeches from the School Presidents. Three boring speeches from the Class Presidents. And three long and boring commencement addresses from the Commencement Speakers.

Here's what I heard.

School Presidents - "Congratulations class of 2012. The faculty and staff are very proud of you. You've reached the mountain top. Don't forget to support your school financially. Blah, blah, blah."

Class Presidents - "We did it. We didn't think this day would ever come. We'd like to thank our family for all their support. Blah, blah, blah."

Commencement Speakers - "Dream big. Challenge yourself. Do good deeds. Make a difference. Blah, blah, blah."

It got so bad at the second one that somebody's grandmother fell and broke her arm so she wouldn't have to suffer through it anymore. I was jealous.

The next graduation I go to, which hopefully will be never, this is what I'd like to hear.

School President - "Congratulations graduates. The faculty and staff are in awe. We don't know how you did it. Obviously, our requirements for making it here aren't tough enough. And don't worry about donating any money to the school. We got so much out of you already that we don't need anymore."

Class President - "Can you believe it? I can't. We didn't want this day to ever come. Why? Because the party's over. I speak for my entire class when I say all we really know how to do is sleep in and drink all day. Will anyone hire us to do that? I didn't think so."

Commencement Speaker - "Do you know why I'm here today? I'll tell you why. Because that guy over there, your School President, is one of my drinking buddies from our fraternity days. Oh, the stories I could tell you about him. Like the one where he showed up to class wearing only his tennis shoes. And then there was the time, ah, maybe I'll save that one for later. Anyway, he said he'd pay me a boat load of money to do this. So here I am. I didn't even write a speech. No one pays attention anyway. And the truth is, I don't even like this place. This school's a joke. But I do want to wish you good luck. You're gonna need it. And with that, I'm out of here."

Blah, blah, blah.

IT IS BRAIN SURGERY!

My wife and I both know the outcome before it ever happens, yet I do it anyway. Sending me to Lowe's or Home Depot to buy stuff is like asking me to perform brain surgery. And in case you're wondering, I'm not a brain surgeon.

These stores are exercises in frustration. First of all, they're too dang big. When you're as clueless as I am, it takes forever to find what you're looking for. And when you finally do, that's when the real confusion sets in. For instance, buying screws should be simple enough right? WRONG!!! Who knew there were 5,000 different kinds? You have drywall screws, wood screws, lag screws, cam screws, connecting screws, machine screws, sheet metal screws. Come on. Are they really all necessary? I don't think so. And what does it mean? What it means is that I'm guaranteed to come home with the wrong ones. And that assures me of another trip back to my favorite store to try again. An added bonus is that I get to stand in long return lines when I go, which only adds to my enjoyment.

Shortly after moving in to our house, we needed towel bars and toilet paper holders. My wife was with me so she couldn't blame this one all on me. When we got home, we discovered they came with drywall screws. We don't have drywall. We have wood. Back I go. What size screws? How the heck do I know? After similar experiences like this, I realized it might be helpful to bring the original screws with me so that at least I'm in the right ballpark. Of course when I get there, I can't figure it out on my own. I play dumb, which is really not an act, and ask a store associate for help. Ok, so now I have the right screws, but they still won't work because the head (and that would be the technical term for the top of the screw) is too small. Now what? Go to the local hardware store and ask them. My wife is in the car but she doesn't want to go in. Oh yeah, I've already demonstrated how incompetent I can be by myself. I'm not about to make another return trip. You're comin' in too. Turns out I need washers to make it work. And thank god it does. Of course, installing them correctly is another story.

You've heard the jokes "How many people does it take to install a light bulb?" Well, the new version is "How many Kevin Engles does it take to buy the correct light bulb?" Yes, even accomplishing this seemingly easy task is far from easy. All you need to know are watts and volts right? Wrong. What was I thinking? Obviously I wasn't. There are different shaped light bulbs. Do you want one with a bent tip or a blunt tip? There are different bases for light bulbs, including a medium base and a candelabra base. Would you like a medium base with an F15 shape? I thought an F15 was a fighter jet? And then you have the so-called "long lasting double life" light bulbs. Do you spend the extra money on those? And do they really last twice as long?

And this is the simple stuff. What about the more complicated things like closet shelving? I'm already dreading that job. I know when I finally muster the courage to tackle that project, one of two things will happen, if not both. Either we won't have the right stuff to do the job, or we won't have enough of the right stuff to get it done. Either way, I'm headed back to my favorite store. I've already named my wife foreman for the project. God knows what it would look like if I did it.

A friend tells me she loves going to these stores. What? How can that be? Is she insane? She does have four kids, so maybe. I'd rather get a tooth pulled. Without Novocain. My pulse races and I get all sweaty. And that's just when I pull into the parking lot. My wife once called the police because she thought I was missing. Turns out I was lost in the lumber aisle. No one could figure out why I was crying. Including myself.

I gotta go. The hospital just paged me. They need me to perform a brain transplant. On myself. It couldn't be any tougher than buying screws and light bulbs.

REALLY?

I'm at work. I'm in the bathroom. I'm doing what you do when you're in the bathroom.

Someone else is too.

When he finishes what he came to do, he heads out the door.

Without washing his hands!

Ok, time out.

When I was a kid, I didn't always wash my hands before leaving the bathroom. Why, I don't know, but I didn't. Kids don't always do what they're supposed to.

Obviously, neither do adults. Maybe this guy has a good excuse. I just can't think what it could be.

He forgot?

I doubt it. And if he did, there are two signs, one on the door and one on the wall by the door, reminding us to wash up.

He doesn't know he's supposed to?

Really? Like he's never heard that a million times before.

He has some kind of phobia to soap or water? Or maybe he's allergic?

Yeah, and women mistake me for George Clooney all the time.

I've seen this guy in action before.

I've heard the water running, but I know he didn't use any soap. You can hear the soap dispenser when someone presses it and I didn't hear that sound. And believe me, I was listening.

Other times, he never even turned on the water.

And when I've been at the sink washing my hands, he had no choice but to do the same, although it was a half-hearted attempt lasting all of two seconds.

I used to make fun of people who'd do just about anything humanly possible to get out of the bathroom without touching the door.

Open it with their foot. Call 911. Or wait for someone else to come along and do it for them.

Now, after seeing Mr. Not-So-Clean, I'm one of them, although I simply opt for the paper towel method.

Maybe I should say something to him?

That would be an interesting conversation.

"Hey buddy, don't take this the wrong way or anything, but I happened to notice that, ah, you didn't wash your hands, you know, before you left the bathroom. I'm sure you just forgot, but since I've seen you do it a bunch of other times, I wanted to let you know how disgusting that is. Have a nice day."

I'm sure he'd take it well, don't you?

The more I think about it, the madder I get. I'm appalled. I'm outraged. I'm also a chicken. What if he hits me? I don't want that. Not with those germ-infested hands.

I'll put a note on his desk when he's not around.

NOT IN MY HOUSE!

Wednesday

9:27PM – My wife and I retire for the evening. We're leaving in the morning to spend a long weekend with family and friends. We need a good night's rest.

11:43 – We both sit up in bed. What's the strange noise coming from the kitchen pantry?

11:43:05 – I jump out of the sack, knowing what I need to do. Sort of. Ok, I've never done this before, but call it instinct. I'm protecting my house and my wife. I grab one of my bedroom slippers. I'd rather not, but I'm willing to sacrifice it for the cause.

11:43:20 – I open the pantry doors but don't see it. I begin emptying the pantry.

11:44 – The culprit, the intruder, the mouse, is spotted, scurrying about hither and thither. My pulse skyrockets.

11:45 – My wife joins me in the kitchen. We quickly hatch a plan. It includes my bedroom slipper and the vacuum cleaner. The vacuum cleaner is plugged in and ready to go.

11:47 – All glass jars are removed from the pantry. The gallon jugs of water are strategically positioned to prevent escape. My pulse is still at an elevated level. I'm confident we'll achieve our goal.

11:49 – Operation Mouse Trap is a go. I hold the vacuum hose with one hand and my bedroom slipper with the other. My wife turns on the vacuum cleaner. Sensing danger, the mouse hides between the wall and one of the water jugs. As I get closer, he jumps. So do I. Somehow he escapes the containment area and runs across the kitchen floor. My wife screams. I curse. We were so close.

Thursday

12:15AM – we return to bed, having reset a trap to catch him alive. PETA would be happy. Sleep is futile. My adrenaline is flowing like a raging river.

12:45 – we again hear strange noises coming from the pantry.

12:50:15 – the trap clicks shut.

12:50:16 – I run to the kitchen, throw open the pantry doors and curse. The trap is empty. The bait gone.

12:59 – I look in the phone book but can't find the number. They're not listed. How can they not be listed? I'm irritated. I track down a receipt and call the number. Yes, they're open and they have the goods.

1:13 – I leave for Walmart. I'm not happy. I don't like to shop. I particularly don't like to shop at 1:13 in the morning.

1:33 – I arrive at Walmart. My mood hasn't gotten any better. I park at the wrong entrance. Only one door is open this time of day.

1:42 – I walk back to my car toting $23.99 in assorted varieties of mouse traps. My wife will know what to use.

2:03 – I arrive home, still not excited how my day is going. I should be counting sheep, not chasing mice.

2:07 – my wife greets me in the kitchen and we begin assessing our mouse catching options.

2:15 – I place three traps in the pantry. They range from the standard old fashioned variety to the ultra-deluxe Taj Mahal version.

2:20:01 – Our uninvited guest enters the Taj Mahal, enticed by the smell of creamy peanut butter.

2:20:02 – the intruder enters mouse heaven.

2:21 – I relocate the Taj Mahal outside, just to be sure there are no more escapes.

2:35 – we set the other traps, in case he was entertaining friends.

2:45 – we go back to bed, pleased with the outcome.

2:50 – I fall asleep.

2:55 – I open one eye. What was that sound?

NEW KNIVES, ANAL AUNTS AND OVEREAGER WAITERS

"How about using a clean knife? Please."

I was at a Subway® restaurant picking up dinner. My wife wanted tuna. After making hers and cutting it in half, the "sandwich artist" was about to use the very same knife, the one with tuna all over it, to cut mine.

That's a no no. A big no no.

I don't care for tuna or anything else that has mayonnaise in it or on it. Potato salad, egg salad, tuna salad, macaroni salad, ham salad. Get it away from me.

I'm picky about what I like and don't like. But I'm not the only one.

My wife doesn't want green peppers on her half of the pizza. She says the taste grows over everything.

She also has a thing about a food's "texture". I don't fully get that one, although I did have some soft squishy grapes the other day and wasn't too wild about those.

When my aunt is at a restaurant, she's extremely particular about how she wants her meal.

"Keep the gravy on the side," she'll tell the waitress. "And don't let the fries touch the pickle. And no ice in my water."

It's embarrassing.

We used to eat out with friends who were agonizingly slow when it came time to order their meals. With the waiter standing there, they'd go over every item on the menu, trying to decide what to get.

"The tilapia sounds good. How's that prepared? Is it spicy? What about the sirloin? Does it have a lot of fat? And the chicken breast? Can I get it without the skin?"

I can only imagine what was going through the waiter's head.

I know what was going through mine.

"Pleeeeeeeeeeeeeeeeeeeeeeeeeeease pick something. I'd like to eat. Tonight."

It was torture. And they did it *every* time.

I appreciate good service, but sometimes the wait staff tries too hard. For instance, I don't necessarily want, or need, my water glass filled every twenty-seven seconds. I like to finish things, but how am I supposed to do that when they keep filling up my glass?

"How is everything?" they'll ask.

Typically, it's before I've even had a chance to take my first bite.

"Give me a minute and I'll let you know."

Do you know any food inspectors with the health department? You probably work with them. They're the people who insist on checking out what you have to eat and are more than willing to sample if you're willing to share.

"Ooooh, what's that?" they ask as they stand behind you, salivating over your meal.

"It's my lunch. Now back off."

If you're starving, I'll share. If you're just curious, go away.

I don't ask for much. A new knife at Subway®, friends who know what they want to eat and an empty water glass.

Bon appétit.

■ ■ ■

The author loves pizza. Without onions. No olives either. And skip the hot peppers.

18 QUESTIONS AND NO RIGHT ANSWERS

Nothing is simple these days.

I wanted to print out our monthly bank statement.

Before I could, I had to track down my username and password. With only about 784 different online accounts, I sometimes have trouble remembering them all.

Ok, got it.

I logged on to the bank's website and typed them in.

Instead of seeing my account information pop up, what I got was a page telling me my security questions had expired. It was time to pick new ones. You know, those questions that are supposed to protect you from hackers getting your stuff?

There were three sets of questions. Six in each group. Eighteen in all. I had to pick one question from each group.

Question #1.

What was your dream job as a child?

Seriously?

I didn't mind cutting grass or taking out the garbage, but I wouldn't consider those a dream job.

Or do you mean what did I want to be when I grew up?

Ok, that makes more sense. I loved playing baseball. How about a professional baseball player?

What was your favorite place to visit as a child?

Do you mean someplace like the beach? Does the Dairy Queen count?

If you could witness any event (past, present or future), what would it be?

My birth?

I don't know.

Question #2.

What is your biggest pet peeve?

That's a tough one. I have a lot of pet peeves. Answering stupid questions like this is high on my list at the moment.

If you could be a character out of any novel, who would you be?

Ahhhhhhhhhhhhhhhhhhhhhhhhhhhh.

What is the first name of your favorite relative not in the immediate family?

That sounds like one of those complicated math questions from junior high school.

If one train leaves San Francisco at 7PM on Wednesday and is traveling at 70mph, while another pulls out of Pittsburgh Thursday morning at 5AM and is moving at 65mph, where will they meet?

Question #3.

Where do you want to retire?

That's a good one. I am retired and my wife and I haven't figured it out. If anyone can tell us where we should retire, and why, that'd be greatly appreciated.

What is the name of your most memorable stuffed animal?

I don't think I ever had a stuff animal. Maybe that's what's wrong with me.

If you won a million dollars, what is the most extravagant purchase you would make?

I don't see that happening since I rarely play the lottery. But if it did, maybe a stuffed animal. One of those really big ones you win at the fair.

And I'd name him Godzilla.

I give up.

From now on, I have a new strategy for answering these stupid security questions.

I'm gonna make stuff up.

Where did your parents meet?

On Mars.

What is the first musical instrument you learned to play?

The bagpipes.

What is your dream car?

A station wagon.

I feel better already, knowing my account is impenetrable. No hacker is gonna get those.

I doubt I'll remember them either.

I'd better jot those down.

NEW SHOES AND NIMBUS CLOUDS

I bought a new pair of running shoes the other day. I didn't really want to but my wife made me. She said I need to take better care of my feet. Throw away my old worn out shoes and get good ones.

She and her brother have been having these conversations about feet and shoes and getting older. According to them, your feet change as you age and you need shoes with more support.

Whatever. I'm sure they're right, but if it meant shelling out a lot of money for new ones, I wasn't too excited.

But that's exactly what she made me do. More than I'd ever spent before.

My previous max had been about 40 bucks. Tell someone that today and they'll laugh at you.

I guess you can't get very good athletic shoes for 40 bucks these days.

And when I was a kid, they were all called 'tennis shoes' whether they were for tennis or not.

The young lady helping me said they should last 300-500 miles. And since I'll be walking in them, not running, maybe more. For what I paid, I hope so.

There's gel in the soles to support my feet and that's supposedly a good thing. I've had toothpaste with gel, but not shoes.

A friend of a friend recommended this particular brand. She's a foot doctor so I guess she should know.

I went to a foot doctor once. He said I had mini-bunions, whatever they are. I wasn't too wild about a guy touching my feet, but they'd been bothering me so I went. It was a weird appointment. He took x-rays and then disappeared into his basement to read them. He was gone a long time. It was strange. I never went back and for the most part ignored what he told me. My feet have been pretty much ok since then.

Anyway, in the store I was looking at different styles with names like Quantum and Cumulus. I went for the Gel Nimbus-17, not the 18. The 17 were a few bucks cheaper than the newer 18.

Those words, cumulus and nimbus, sounded vaguely familiar.

And then I remembered why.

They're clouds. Those white things you see up in the sky. Not the places where computer companies store our files these days.

I guess when you wear these shoes, it's like you're walking on a cloud.

Really? And how would they know?

I looked at the company's website today. They have different shoes for just about every sport out there. Running, walking, training, wrestling, volleyball, golf, and yes, even tennis. And there were words I'd barely heard before, words you probably only say in foot doctor's offices and shoe stores. Strange terms like over and underpronators and shock attenuation. Turns out overpronation means flat feet. I have heard of that.

When I told the sales associate I was getting soreness in my foot and showed her where, she said that was the ball of my foot.

Ok, I probably should've known that.

She said my new Gel Nimbus-17 running shoes would be good for the balls of my feet.

I hope so.

What I do know is I paid a lot of money for them and won't be satisfied unless I'm walking on a cloud.

And I don't care what kind.

As long as it's light and fluffy.

DEAD BATTERIES AND FULL BLADDERS

My wife heard it first.

She nudged me, but I was out of it, lost in dream land.

"Chirp."

She nudged me again.

Still no response. When I'm asleep, really asleep, it takes a minor earthquake to get my attention.

"CHIRP!"

I jumped as that registered on my Richter scale.

The smoke alarm battery was dying. The one in our bedroom.

I rubbed my eyes and squinted at the red numbers on the alarm clock.

3:15.

Why do these things always happen in the middle of the night?

"We'd better change that," my wife said.

"Now?" I asked, not wanting to.

Have you ever woken up and had to go to the bathroom, like now, but were too lazy to do it?

That's what this was like.

Maybe I could ignore it.

Maybe I wouldn't hear it again.

Maybe it would go back to sleep.

And maybe my elected officials truly have my best interests in mind.

Yeah.

"Chirp."

"CHIRP!"

"#$%^*$##!" I grumbled as my feet hit the floor.

Changing the smoke alarm battery in our bedroom is a two person job. And since there was no one else around to help my wife, I guess that meant me.

That smoke alarm is more than eleven feet off the floor. We need a ladder. That ladder is in the garage. I can't get to that ladder unless I first back my car out of the garage. And if I carry that ladder up the stairs myself, I'll be banging it in to the walls.

I threw on my sweatpants, grabbed my car keys and headed for the garage.

I opened the garage door.

I backed the car out.

We lifted the ladder off the wall and carefully negotiated it up the stairs, around a few bends and into our room, setting it down on some old rugs my wife had strategically positioned on the floor.

We didn't dare get dirt on the floor. Even in the middle of the night.

Ok, that's my rule.

To my surprise, I replaced the battery and screwed the smoke alarm back on without any issues, something I typically can't do in the middle of the day, let alone the middle of the night.

At 3:45, we climbed back into bed.

I was asleep two and a half seconds later.

"Chirp."

I lay there, my eyes open, expecting to hear it again.

But that was it. For some reason, it always does that after we replace the battery.

I closed my eyes.

And then I remembered.

I still had to go to the bathroom.

"#$%^*$##!"

HOW TO TURN 52¢ INTO $200

I did it.

And you can too.

In just a few easy steps.

Here's how.

I got an email from Best Buy. There was a $10 coupon in it.

Great, except that it was only good for the next two days.

Crap. I hate when they do that.

After thinking about it rationally, I decided not to get anything.

There'd be another $10 coupon in my future.

The next day, when I reread the email, I couldn't resist.

I just can't let a good coupon go to waste.

And I already knew what I wanted.

The Martian, a movie that was on my Christmas list. I thought for sure my wife would get it for me.

I went online and found it.

And to save a few bucks in shipping, I'd pick it up myself the next time I was out.

The $10 off covered all but 52¢.

You gotta love that.

After clicking "Submit" to finalize the sale, I received a confirmation. I was to pick it up within the next 10 days.

No problem, except we were going out of town and I didn't feel like making a special trip to the store before we left just to get it.

I called customer service and requested an extension.

Sure thing.

When we got back from our trip, I still didn't feel like going to the store, but knew I had to.

I persuaded my wife to come along for the ride. We could take care of some other things as well.

And that's when the magic began.

First stop, Michaels, the craft store. She needed yarn for one of her projects and I snagged two picture frames as well. Fifty-seven bucks.

Next. Bed Bath & Beyond. With coupon in hand, she purchased a drying mat for the kitchen. Twelve dollars.

Lunch at Chick-fil-A just down the road. Nine more George Washingtons.

And then to Best Buy to pick up that 52¢ movie. And Turbo Tax. And iPhone adapters. $123.

Dessert at the Dairy Queen. It was in the neighborhood. You don't get that close to a DQ and not stop. Two Butterfinger® Blizzards®. Just four bucks thanks to a buy one get one free coupon.

And finally, two Papa John's pizzas to take home. Twenty-two dollars more.

Total damages?

Two hundred twenty-seven smackeroos.

And that's how I turned a 52¢ purchase into more than $200 on my credit card.

It was easy.

Too easy.

But I did learn an important lesson that day.
Next time, pay for the shipping.
It'll save us a lot of money.

¢¢¢¢¢¢¢¢¢¢¢¢¢¢¢¢¢¢¢¢¢¢¢¢¢¢

The author wished his bank could turn 52¢ into $200 in a day.
Wouldn't that be nice?

PART FOUR

People

MAKING THE WORLD A SAFER PLACE, ONE MILE AT A TIME

My wife is a better driver than me. I know it. She knows it. And now so do you.

But I'm a lucky guy, because that means I have a personal driving instructor, one who's more than willing to share her expertise with me anytime I want it. And even when I don't.

"You're getting too close to that car."

"I see brake lights ahead. You'd better slow down."

"Are you paying attention to the speed limit?"

"Are you paying attention?"

That's how it used to be whenever I was behind the wheel.

But not anymore.

Not since we've adopted the BDP.

The Better Driving Program.

You see, I respond best to positive reinforcement, and that's what the BDP is all about. Designed by both of us, it rewards me for good driving behavior while also taking into account the times when I mess up.

For example, if I can keep it between the lines, I earn one point.

If I stay within five miles of the speed limit, that's another point.

Don't run any red lights and I get two more.

Not cursing at any of my fellow drivers, three points.

And the biggie, maintaining my composure when the jerk beside me cuts me off. Five points. I'm still working on that one.

If I do slip up, infractions become deductions.

Run a red light, minus two points, etc.

Obviously, the goal is to make me a better driver. But beyond that, there are tangible rewards as well.

Whenever I reach 100 points, I can go to the mall and get a Cinnabon. Extra frosting is another five points.

Two hundred points and I'm playing nine holes of golf.

And the ultimate BDP reward? Five hundred points and I get a "No chore Saturday".

We were in Washington D.C. recently, trying to find our way to a parking garage.

"What's that?" I asked as I spotted a large building I'd not seen before.

"I don't know," my wife replied without looking. "Just keep your eyes on the road."

Minus two points.

"What's going on over there?" I wondered when I saw a crowd of people carrying flags and walking around.

My wife sighed.

Another deduction.

"Whoa!" I said as I hit the brakes to avoid the car in front of me. "Didn't see that coming."

Minus five.

My driving instructor was not pleased.

And neither was I. I wouldn't be having Cinnabons any time soon. And I didn't see my golf game improving much either.

At least I'll be getting a lot done around the house.

■ ■ ■

Mr. Engle will soon be talking with his wife about something she may be interested in. The BCP. The Better Cooking Program. Then again, maybe now's not the time.

IF YOU CAN'T BEAT THEM, ...

I have one.

So do you.

Every neighborhood does.

That one person who's always a step ahead of you. No matter what it is, he or she gets it done before you and better than you. Their grass is greener, their car cleaner and their tomato plants taller.

In most neighborhoods, you know them as the Joneses, and no matter what you do, you can't keep up with them.

Where I live, it's a woman and I call her Rambo. She attacks everything with the precision and skill of a highly trained special forces military unit. For all I know, she probably helped take down that bin Laden guy. Wouldn't surprise me.

Every spring, when I realize the lawn doesn't fertilize itself, Rambo's already knocked that one out several weeks ago.

And when I don't see my riding tractor cutting the grass on its own, Rambo's done hers three times.

"I can't cut it now," I tell my wife. "It's raining. I'll get wet."

And then I hear it. The unmistakable sound ... of the Rambo tractor!

"Dang her!"

When it comes to washing the car, she does it every weekend. Me, I take a more relaxed approach. Once every 100,000 miles.

In the fall, when I can't see my lawn because of the two million leaves covering it, Rambo's already tackled her yard with a gas-powered blower.

And when the snow starts piling up on the driveway, and my wife suggests, for the fifth time, that I might want to see how well the snow blower works, Rambo's putting hers back in the garage. I've even heard her out there in the middle of the night. Does that take a lot of nerve or what? Some of us like to sleep at that hour.

I wonder if she realizes how annoying she really is? I wonder if she cares? I should tell her. Then again, I'll have my wife do it.

Speaking of my wife, she didn't want me to write this.

"What if she reads it?"

"So what if she does?" I replied. "She doesn't scare me. What's she gonna do? Take me out like bin Laden?"

"Well," my wife said nervously as she glanced out the window toward Rambo's recently power washed house. "You never know."

After much soul searching, and cursing, I finally realized this was a no win situation. I'm never gonna get the best of Rambo. It just ain't gonna happen.

To be honest, now that I've said it, I feel better. I no longer feel like I have to compete with her. In fact, I'm going to do the next best thing.

You know what they say? If you can't beat them, hire them.

THE THREE BIG ONES

My wife is a stretcher. She stretches her muscles by practicing yoga and Pilates. She stretches her mind by reading books. And unfortunately for me, she stretches the truth, at my expense. She has three favorites that she's repeatedly used on me over the years. I call them the Three Big Ones. You might even be familiar with them.

Number one. "It won't take long."

She utters these seemingly harmless words every time we begin a home repair or home improvement project. I've come to despise those words. When it comes to mechanical abilities, my wife and I are complete opposites. She has them and I don't. Remember the TV show *MacGyver*? The lead character could do just about anything. Give him a safety pin, chewing gum and duct tape, and look out. My wife is the same way. I'm more like Mr. Magoo, the blind bumbling cartoon character. Add to that my lack of patience and low frustration level, and you've got a bad mix. And of course, every project we tackle takes longer than it should. The easy job that was supposed to take an hour requires all afternoon. The all day jobs take all weekend. And yet, my lovely wife has the audacity, the nerve, to say it again the next time. "It won't take long." I don't believe her any more.

Truth stretcher.

Number two. "It won't take me long."

I hear this one when she's in the bathroom getting ready. It doesn't matter where we're going or what time of the day it is, she'll be late. I hate to be late. If my life depended on it, I couldn't tell you what she's doing in there. She doesn't wear a lot of makeup, so that can't be it. Her hair is fairly short and she doesn't blow dry it, so that's out too. I don't know what's occupying her time, but there's something going on in the bathroom. And then, when she's almost done, she'll say it will just be another minute or two. That's wifespeak for five. At least.

Truth stretcher.

Number three. "It won't cost much."

Really? My wife doesn't like to go to the mall. That's every husband's dream isn't it? But who needs the mall when you get truckloads of catalogs delivered right to your mailbox? She looks through catalogs more often than I look through the refrigerator, and I like to snack. Sure, maybe the seat cushions for the back porch aren't all that expensive, but let's not forget about the drying racks for the laundry room. And the lamps for the great room. And plates for the kitchen. And bath towels. And a refrigerator for the basement. It never ends. Every time she picks up a catalog, I can hear the cha-ching of a cash register in some other state. "Don't worry," she assures me, "it won't cost much."

Truth stretcher.

It's ironic. My wife is the stretcher, but that's what they'll carry me out of the house on the next time I hear one of the Three Big Ones.

NO INTERRUPTIONS!

"Listen to this," my wife said as she began reading an email aloud.

"Not now, I'm watching *SURVIVOR*™," I told her, as if she didn't already know that. After all, she was sitting two feet away.

"You won't believe what happened at work today," she began.

"Not now, I'm watching *SURVIVOR*™," I repeated.

"Here's that sweater you've been wanting to buy," she said as she held out the latest L.L. Bean catalog for me to look at. "It's on sale."

"Shhhhhhhhhhhhh!"

I was getting annoyed. After all, I was watching *SURVIVOR*™. And so was she. Besides, she knows better. We've had this conversation before. When *SURVIVOR*™ is on, there are to be NO INTERRUPTIONS. You don't answer the phone, you don't have a meaningful conversation, nothing. The only thing I want to do when *SURVIVOR*™ is on is watch *SURVIVOR*™. That's not entirely true. I can stuff my face full of popcorn as well, but that doesn't count.

My wife, like a lot of women, are excellent multitaskers. Isn't that what you have to be today to stay on top of stuff? Do 25 things at once? I'm not like that. In fact, I'm just the opposite. I excel at uni-tasking. One thing at a time. And I'm proud of it.

When I'm watching TV, that's what I want to do. Watch TV. I don't want to surf the net, send emails, read the paper, talk on the phone or look through a catalog. I want to watch TV.

Is that such a bad thing?

My wife, on the other hand, can do all that stuff and more. Sometimes she forgets my limitations and expects me to be like her. Ain't happenin'.

When I'm behind the wheel, I don't like to talk on the phone. I have a hard enough time staying focused on my driving as it is. I don't need a phone conversation to distract me as well. When I was in college and had school work to do, I'd hide out in the library until I got it done. It's just the way I'm built.

There is one place where the tables are turned. One place where I can multitask, and do it quite well. My wife, on the other hand, wants no part of it.

And where would that be?

In the bathroom.

Like a lot of guys, I like to read while taking care of my business. Kill two birds with one stone so the saying goes.

I wonder if I could fit a TV in there as well?

THE BRITISH ARE COMING! THE BRITISH ARE COMING!

They're not really British. I don't think so.

Some friends are coming over, for dinner.

And we have to get ready.

It's their first time to the house.

And we want to make a good impression.

If it's someone who's been here before, you don't care as much.

But first timers?

You don't want them to think you're slobs.

Not that we are, but we're not always as neat as we should be.

And that's why we're in clean up mode.

We have been for the last few days.

Do you know what the worst thing is about having people over to the house?

It's getting ready to have people over to the house.

It's exhausting.

Cleaning and dusting and vacuuming. Mopping the basement floor. Shaking the floor mats. Picking up stuff and putting it away. Stuff that shouldn't be where it is. The stack of newspapers and catalogs on the floor. Three days of mail on the kitchen counter.

Shoes scattered about in the basement. Coupons on top of my dresser instead of in my dresser.

All that and we still have to make dinner.

I'm worn out before they ever get here.

I shouldn't complain. My wife does most of the work. But I do anyway. I'm good at it.

I help, some, but not enough.

I don't mind vacuuming, and I actually like to wash windows, but I'm not big on dusting. Or cleaning the commodes.

She gets that job.

And when she's done in the spare bathroom, which also includes putting out the nice decorative towels that never see the light of day any other time, she has a warning for me.

"Stay out!"

I'm not even allowed to *look* in that bathroom let alone use it.

But it's my favorite.

There's a window next to the commode. On a sunny day, I can sit there and read without even turning on a light. It's a great place to go when you gotta go. Much better than in the master bathroom where the commode is stuck in a dark corner.

Once the house is clean enough, we turn our attention to the food.

We decided on the menu a few days ago and I picked up everything from the store.

We're not great cooks, but we can put together a decent meal.

During the week, if it's just us and we want something quick and easy, we'll throw frozen dinners in the oven or microwave. Food in a bag or fish in a box as I like to call it.

But not for company.

You want to go that extra step and actually make something for them. Something that requires a little more effort.

And hope they like it.

And aren't allergic.
Yeah, having people over is a lot of work.
We'd be better off if the British were coming.
We could do takeout. Fish and chips from Long John Silvers.
That's quick and easy.
Just the way we like it.

■ ■ ■

The author likes Long John Silvers. His wife? She's not a big fan.

UNWANTED – DEAD OR ALIVE!

I glanced at my wife. She could see my pain. She could feel my pain.

I mumbled the words "grocery store" and headed for the door. She knew why.

We had a problem. Unwanted house guests. And they were in no hurry to leave.

If they weren't going, I was.

The first step in dealing with unwanted house guests, like so many other things, is prevention. Discourage them from coming in the first place. Tell them about the rare and contagious disease you've contracted. The one with no cure.

"You can still visit," you say, "but you'll have to wear contamination suits to protect yourself."

That one works well.

Or casually mention the nightmares, and the blood curdling screams at 3AM.

"Just ignore it," you laugh. "You might not even hear me."

Or that you have to go out of town for work. Even if you are unemployed.

We'd been successful in holding them off for several years, but in a moment of weakness, coupled with guilt and stupidity, we gave in. Plus, we'd run out of good excuses.

Now what?

Phase 2. Make them feel as uncomfortable and unwelcome as you can, while trying to be pleasant about it.

"This is your room," you say and then toss their stuff on the floor. "There shouldn't be any more bed bugs. But just in case, you might want to use the special soap we bought. The label says it's 50% effective."

That usually shortens the stay.

Or, "We've had a little problem with rats, but I think we got the last one this morning. Right under your bed as a matter of fact. Sweet dreams."

"They'll be gone by morning," I whispered.

I was wrong.

And now, when they were supposed to leave, they were in no hurry.

I was desperate. This had never happened before. I didn't know what to do. There was no Phase 3.

My survival instincts kicked in. Choosing between fight or flight, I flew. And so off to the grocery store I went. An hour later, when I was done, I headed for home. My gut told me they'd still be there.

I had two choices. Pull off somewhere and wait for the "all clear" call from my wife. Or go back, and tough it out. For some unknown reason, probably the stress, I chose to tough it out. I obviously wasn't thinking clearly.

"I can do this!" I said aloud, trying to pump myself up. I felt a surge of adrenaline rushing through my body. And with every left and right turn I made, I could feel my heart beating faster.

And then, I saw it. A sight that brought a smile to my face.

Their car, and it was coming toward me.

They waved.

I waved.

I smiled.

I had survived.

A TIME WE'D LIKE TO FORGET

And as hard as we've tried, we can't.

The memories of those few days, as unpleasant as they were, are burned into our brain like a cattle brand.

December 28th, 1994.

It's my last day of work for the year. My brother and his family are coming tomorrow from out of town. We'll celebrate the New Year together.

I'm sitting at my desk, working, or trying to. I don't feel good. I'm feverish. My head is spacy. I'm very sleepy. I can't concentrate. I put my head down for a minute to rest. I should just go home.

Bad weather is on the way and my employer lets everyone leave a few hours early.

A coworker who lives nearby gives me a ride to my car in the neighborhood park and ride lot. It's a good thing because I don't think I could've gotten there on my regular route, public transportation.

I immediately fall into a deep sleep as he drives. He wakes me when we get there.

I pull in the driveway and drag myself into the house.

Guess who else isn't feeling well?

It hit my wife at the grocery store.

We're both coming down with the flu.

December 29th.

After a good night's rest, we're feeling some better, but not 100%.

I talk to my sister-in-law on the phone.

"We can come another time," she says. "When you're up to it."

My wife thinks that's an excellent idea.

"We'll be fine," I tell my sister-in-law. "C'mon down."

December 30th.

We go out to lunch. Afterwards, we walk around the Civil War era town and check things out.

My youngest nephew, Zach, he's eight, gets mad about something. We're all walking one way and he decides to stomp off in the other direction. By himself.

And he keeps going.

My brother John knows his son isn't about to turn around anytime soon. At eight years old, Zach has a stubborn streak. If John wants his son back, he'd better go get him.

That night, at our house, we're all playing a board game. We thought it'd be fun and a good way to keep the kids entertained.

It didn't quite work out that way.

Zach gets mad. Again. This time it's directed at his older brother Wes.

He stands and screams, "I'll shoot your head off!"

We all just look at each other wide-eyed wondering where that came from.

Ah, brotherly love.

December 31st.
The plan is to drive into Washington D.C. and check out the sights.

My wife can't do it. She's feeling cruddy. Yesterday did her in. I'm not feeling much better than her, but I don't want to send my family off to D.C. by themselves.

"They need a tour guide," I tell myself.

"I'll go with them," I say to my wife. "I'll be fine."

The day is dark and dreary and damp.

The weather that is, although I'm about the same.

Not the perfect time to be out when you have the flu.

We walked for miles, from Arlington Cemetery into D.C. and all around.

I don't know how I did it.

I should've stayed home with my wife.

January 1st.
They leave.

The second they're out the door, we collapse on the couch and stare at each other. For hours. We can't move. We've got nothin' left.

What just happened?

20+ Years Later.
Even today, when one of us brings it up, I get the shakes.

At least we can laugh about it.

Barely.

WEAR IT!

I'm not the most observant guy in the world, but I'm reasonably confident I would've noticed on our first date if my future wife had 78 feet. From all indications, I could only see two.

Flash forward to now.

If she doesn't have 78 feet, then why does she own 39 pair of shoes? I know she can't wear them all at once.

Ok, I understand women, and men, need different shoes for different occasions.

Shoes for work. Shoes for dress up. Shoes for play. Shoes for the beach. Whatever.

But 39 pair?

I was in the closet the other day looking for something when I spotted her shoe rack propped up against the wall. I took a good long look. Sixteen of the eighteen spots were taken.

"How many shoes does she have?" I wondered.

And that's when I did a count. As it turns out, she could open up her own store.

"You can't count flip flops," she said. "They're not shoes."

Ok, I'll give her that, although technically, they are footwear.

My wife owns 38 pair of shoes.

That's a lot.

They say you spend approximately 1/3 of your life sleeping. My wife spends about the same amount of time shoe shopping.

If she's on line, there's a good chance that's what she's doing.

And when she turns off the computer, she's flipping through the shoe catalogs that came in the mail.

We were out the other day and passed by a shoe store.

"Do you want to check it out?" I foolishly asked.

Of course she did. You don't walk by a shoe store and not go in.

Like a good and obedient husband, I waited outside.

How many shoes does one woman possibly need? And how often can you shop for them before you can't take it anymore? You'd think she'd be tired of it by now. I am.

My wife admits she doesn't wear all 39 pair of shoes in her collection. Excuse me, all 38 pair. In fact, it's been years for some of them and she intends to get rid of those.

I'm glad to hear it, but three more boxes arrived last week. Two of them went back for various reasons. And this weekend, her best friend is coming to town. Guess what they'll be doing?

It's really true what they say, and my wife is living proof of it. If the shoe fits, …

■ ■ ■

Mrs. Engle took an inventory as well. By her count, her husband must have 44 feet. ☺

LOVE THY NEIGHBOR

Hey what's your name,

So you really are moving huh?

Job transfer.

That's too bad.

I know you're not thrilled about it.

With a great neighbor like me, I totally understand.

You've been here ever since we moved in. Almost ten years ago.

I'm gonna miss all your expert lawn care advice.

"Use the gray bag for the bugs. And the green bag to fertilize. Try some lime too."

I did all that. And you know what happened? Not a dang thing. My yard still looks like crap.

I'm gonna miss hearing your eardrum-blasting leaf blower. The one that tosses kids and small dogs around like an F-1 tornado.

I'm gonna miss my wife asking why our cars aren't as clean and shiny as yours. That's easy. Because you were obsessed, washing them every weekend. I'm on the annual plan myself.

And with the holidays approaching, you always took great pride in decorating outside. I'm gonna miss seeing the Christmas lights draped around the pine trees in your front yard. They looked so festive every December and January. By March, not so much.

I'm gonna miss all that peer pressure too. You were out snow blowing before the first snowflake landed on your driveway, no matter how cold it was. I got frostbite thanks to you.

And those nasty things you said about my broom? Sure, it's not the prettiest looking, but it gets the job done. The same goes for those comments you were about to make regarding my torn pants. Didn't your mom teach you that "if you can't say anything nice ..." thing?

You were a decent neighbor. Especially when you stayed on your side on the street. Unfortunately, that wasn't often enough.

You did drag that dead deer off our property when we were on vacation. Yeah, I guess I do appreciate that. My wife would've had to take care of it when we got home.

And you always kept us informed about what was going on in the neighborhood. Somehow you were smack in the middle of everything, like you caused it. Did you?

And those great chocolate chip cookies you bragged about? I'll never know since you didn't share any with us.

Yeah, I'm pretty broken up about you moving.

Let us know when you're back in the area visiting.

I'll be gone that day.

Give us your new address so we can send a Christmas card.

Yeah. You bet.

■ ■ ■

His parents did teach him that "if you can't say anything nice ..." thing, but Mr. Engle chooses to ignore it most of the time.

TO DO, TO DO, TO DO

She's been warning me.

For months.

She told me this day would come.

It's here.

She said she'd drive me crazy.

And boy is she.

For the past two years, I've been home.

Alone.

Monday through Friday, while my wife went off to work each day, I spent my time, unsupervised, doing my own thing. Whatever my thing was.

I had my routine. My schedule. My way of doing stuff.

When I cut the grass. When I did errands. When I goofed off on the computer.

Those days are gone.

My wife recently retired.

And my whole world has been turned upside down.

And inside out.

And sideways.

Plus any other direction you can think of.

I love my wife.

But like Frank Sinatra, I like doing things my way.

Kiss those days goodbye.

You're supposed to ease into retirement. Make a smooth transition.

My wife isn't easing into anything.

She's like an F1 tornado who won't stop.

And I'm the collateral damage.

She's making a To Do List.

It's currently three pages long.

Three pages!

And growing.

Of course, her To Do list magically becomes my To Do list.

I get "recruited" to help, whether I want to or not.

And typically, I don't. Especially when I'm in the middle of doing something very important. Like napping.

"I only need you for a few minutes," she'll say pleadingly.

We all know how that turns out.

What's on that To Do List?

Buying shelves for the garage.

Installing shelves in the garage.

Getting more shelves for the pantry.

Installing shelves in the pantry.

Buying new lamps.

Taking sewing machines to be fixed.

Going through boxes and closets to get rid of stuff. Books, papers, clothes, et cetera, et cetera, et cetera.

There's this project, and that one, and a hundred more after that.

I can't take it.

I can't afford it.

I'm trying to teach her to slow down. To learn the beauty of a very important word.

Inexperienced retiree (i.e. my wife) : "I'm going to do, to do, to do, today, today, today."

Wise retiree (i.e. me) : "You can't get all that done today. There's always TOMORROW."

I love that word.

She's going to wear me out.

I need to get in better shape just to keep up.

As it turns out, I already am.

She has a new exercise plan too.

We're up before dawn several days a week walking 3 ½ miles.

And now my knees and legs are sore all the time. I'm hobbling around the house like an old man.

I'm not an old man.

Yet.

But I'm quickly feeling like one.

We're eating oatmeal for breakfast. Oatmeal! I never ate oatmeal for breakfast.

Something's gotta give, and I hope it's not just my knees.

Maybe I should go back to work. Get a part-time job.

.... nah, it's not that bad.

Not yet anyway.

■ ■ ■

Next up on his wife's To Do list? Repair window screens. The author will start on that real soon. Maybe tomorrow?

A BETTER PLACE

My brother John spent a lot of his teenage years running.

Not from the law, but helping others.

No matter what time it was, day or night, he'd tear off when the local volunteer fire department alarm came in. He also spent many hours training and responding to medical emergencies with the ambulance crew.

Last year, he got hooked up with the Make-A-Wish foundation, and through his local chapter, hiked with them for their semi-annual event to raise funds.

And we're not just talking your average stroll in the woods.

One Saturday this past May, he and 80 others hiked 28.3 miles. In one day!

Yeah.

As a show of brotherly support, I walked 10 ½ miles that same day, up and down the hilly streets of a nearby neighborhood. I was so sore that I could barely climb in my car to drive home.

Since May, he's been serving as a hike leader, helping others get in shape for their fall fundraiser.

And today, his youngest son Zach, an optometrist, is in Thailand. He and a team of other eye doctors will spend the next two weeks riding elephants and providing eye care to those who need it but can't afford it.

Neat stuff.

There are many ways we can make the world a better place, and those are just a few examples.

I wrote recently about all the trash I find along the road in front of our house, including one completely wrapped Burger King® cheeseburger my wife wouldn't let me eat.

I mentioned a guy I often see on our road, in his fluorescent vest, picking up that trash.

A friend told me his name is Skip.

Thanks Skip for doing what you do.

And to Martha, one of my wife's former coworkers and friends. She and her husband don their fluorescent vests and do the same thing somewhere in Texas.

Every year around the holidays, we stop by my old neighborhood to visit a family I grew up with. It doesn't seem like Christmas unless we sit down with whoever's there and catch up on each other's lives, even if it's only for an hour or so.

Rosemary, the mom, even in her 80s, is a dynamo. She stays busy helping at church and doing other volunteer work. Her schedule is so packed full it tires me out just hearing about it.

I have a relative who's just like her. Hattie Jean, who's almost 90, is always running from helping at one church event to another. I don't know how she does it.

Technically, she doesn't run. She has a bad knee.

But you get the point.

I did some volunteer work last year but didn't find it all too fulfilling. It's time I found something that is.

Did you know there are people who go out into farmers' fields, with their permission of course, and pick the less-than-perfect but still-fine-to-eat food and send it off to food banks?

I think that's awesome.

I have a soft spot for charities dealing with hunger. Maybe I'll give that a try.

And if I get hungry, it'd be safer to eat than that cheeseburger I found.

So get out there, and make the world a better place, in whatever way you can.

PART FIVE

Just My Imagination

DOES ANYBODY LIKE ME?

My wife says I'm paranoid. Maybe I am. I'll tell you what happened the other day and you can decide for yourself.

Ever get the feeling people are talking about you, whispering as you walk by and giving you strange looks, like something's wrong, but you don't know what it is? That happened to me at work. Was my hair on fire? Had my pants fallen down? I did a quick inspection. Everything seemed to be in order. Ok, what's up with that?

On the way home, I stopped for Chinese takeout. I was hungry for chow mein. The girl behind the counter wasn't all that friendly, but when the next customer walked in, she instantly transformed into a nice person. What did I do? And when my order was ready, she looked in the bag, smirked, and handed it to me. What was that about?

Have you ever had someone give you a dirty look when they passed you on the road? How about a dog? I'm not kidding. This pooch was sitting in the passenger seat of a pickup truck as it passed me. The canine looked my way and cast an evil eye! C'mon, I love dogs.

As I slowed to make a turn, I saw a police car parked on the side of the road facing me. I thought I recognized the guy behind the wheel and so I waved. And you know what he did? He flipped me the finger! That's right. A cop shot me the bird.

I stopped to pick up the mail, just like I do every other day. There was one lonely envelope in the box. It was from a credit card company, no doubt offering me another Visa or Mastercard that I don't want or need, even if I could earn points toward fabulous vacations to the moon. Needless to say, I was a bit surprised when I opened the envelope and read the letter.

"Mr. Engle, do NOT apply for a credit card with our bank. Don't waste your time or ours. We don't want you as a customer. Not today, not tomorrow, never. Got it?"

What the?

When my wife got home, we sat down to eat. I could almost taste that chow mein. I'd been looking forward to it all day. As it turned out, I'd be waiting longer. The girl behind the counter gave me the wrong order. No doubt on purpose.

After eating spicy Chinese food that didn't agree with me, I opened my fortune cookie and shook my head.

"You're a loser and your personality stinks."

"What?" I grabbed another one.

"Just kidding. But you do have bad breath."

"You try," I said to my wife as I handed her one.

"Oh my," she said as she read it to herself and placed it on the table.

I grabbed the little white piece of paper to see for myself.

"You'll find true happiness ... when you divorce that loser."

It was time to call dad. He always knows just what to say to make me feel better.

"Hey dad, you're not gonna believe the day I've had."

Click.

Does anybody like me?

WHAT WOULD YOU DO?

It happened to me. It could happen to you. If it did, what would you do?

Story #1: You're at the grocery store. You see a little girl. She's about six or seven. She reaches into a bag of green grapes on the display case and plops one into her mouth. Mom and dad don't say a word.

What would you do?

A. You scream "Grape stealer!" as loud as you possibly can while shaking your finger at her.
B. You pull out your cell phone and call the produce police.
C. "Excuse me," you say to mom or dad, "you're going to pay for that right?"
D. "Hey, was that good?" you ask and then do the same thing.

My gut reaction was A, then B, followed by C, but I was hungry. I didn't have enough for breakfast. And to answer my own question, yes, the grapes were quite tasty. Between the two of us, we finished the whole bag. Next time, I'm going for the apples.

Story #2: You pull into the gas station to fill up. It's quite busy. All the pumps are in use and there's a line at most of them. You spot a motorcycle at the last one. Knowing that it won't take as long for the bike to gas up, you pull behind it. Biker Dude is standing there talking on the phone while Biker Chick is sitting in front of the pump and appears to be texting. You notice the hose is not inserted into the bike's gas tank. Thus, no gasoline is moving from the pump to the motorcycle. Biker Dude and Biker Chick wave you on.

"Is the pump not working?"

"Our motorcycle's broken down."

"Can you push it out of the way?" you ask, thinking that's a perfectly reasonable request.

"We're working on it," Biker Chick says without looking up. And without missing a beat, she continues to text and/or surf the net.

Hmm. You wonder if they really are working on it.

What would you do?

A. You blow the horn, wave your arms like a madman and gun it, pushing their bike out of the way. And then you fill up.

B. "It's rather busy here. I'm sure everyone waiting would appreciate if you moved a little faster."

C. You get out of your car and politely offer to help them move the bike.

D. You do as they ask and swing around to another pump, gritting your teeth as you pull to the back of the line.

I considered D, but immediately decided against it. I then went B followed by A. I was in a hurry. And a bit short on patience.

Story #3: You get to work and park beside another car. The driver gets out, walks around to the passenger side, opens his door and mumbles something. You don't catch it at first, but then it hits you.

"whole parking lot …. right beside me. Whole parking lot …. right beside me."

Mr. Grumpy is not happy that you chose to park next to him when you could have parked somewhere else.

What would you do?

A. "I'm sorry," you tell him. "You're right. That was thoughtless of me. I'll park in another spot." And then you do.

B. "You big jerk! I didn't realize this was your personal parking lot. Get a life loser."

C. The next time you see him, which will be tomorrow because now you're on the lookout, you pull two inches away from his driver side door and get a friend to do the same thing on the passenger side. If he wants in, his only option is through the trunk.

D. You laugh it off and give him the benefit of the doubt. We all have bad days right?

I wasn't in the mood for A or D and opted for B and C instead. What can I say? That's just the kind of guy I am.

A VERY COLORFUL CONVERSATION

A guy walks into a bar.

Red: Well look who's here.

Me: Hey, I don't want any trouble. Just a root beer.

Red: You don't want any trouble? Really? I should pour that root beer over your head. Why are you so nasty to us? We never did anything to you.

Me: What are you talking about?

Red: What am I talking about? Seriously? You ride around on that lawn tractor of yours and mulch us up into smithereens.

Me: I could burn you in a barrel, like my neighbor does.

Red: No, no, don't do that! Please.

Me: I know the real you. You're all just a bunch of trouble makers. People look at you and think you're so beautiful.

Red: We are beautiful.

Me: I'll give you that. But then it gets ugly. You and your friends falling all over the place. In my yard. On my driveway. Clogging my gutters. Why do you do it?

Red: Calm down dude. Chill, like the temperature. It's what we do. That's all I know.

Me: You're obviously not the smartest leaf on the tree. What about you two? What do you have to say?

Yellow: Red's right. It's what we do. We hang out for a few months, but then something happens. It must be in our DNA.

Orange: Actually Yellow, it's our chlorophyll, but you were close.

Yellow: Whatever. All I know is I was Green a few weeks ago. Heck, all of us were Green. Now look at me.

Orange: You're stunning. We all are.

Yellow: But something tells me I'm going on a trip soon. And I keep having this same dream I'm falling. I don't like to fly.

Orange: Oh Yellow. You know how Mama Bird kicks Baby Bird out of the nest? Well, Tree is about to tell us to take a hike, or fly, whichever you prefer.

Yellow: I'd prefer to stay right where I am.

Orange: I know, I know.

Red: Think of it as surfing. That's what I do. Instead of a wave, we're catchin' air. Just ride that air wave all the way down to this guy's yard.

Me: Tell me this. Why can't you get it over with all at one time? Why do you have to drag it out? This goes on for weeks.

Red: You need to take your blood pressure meds man. You're all wound up.

Me: You would be too if you spent day after day cleaning up after the three of you.

Yellow: Why don't you just sweep us up like you used to and drag us into the woods? We got to hang out with all our friends and stay nice and warm in those big piles.

Me: I'll tell you why, because that was double the work. It's a lot faster to grind you into dust.

Red: If we bought you a root beer, can we talk about it?

Me: Make it two, and we'll see what happens.

To be continued …

■ ■ ■

The author doesn't really talk to leaves. Well, not that often.

LOWER, SLOWER AND BIGGER

Dear International Olympic Committee:

I know you're real busy right now getting ready for the Beijing Olympics, but I have a great idea I need to tell you about. If you'd like to make the Olympic games even more popular than they already are, and rake in more money than you already do from the television networks, I have a few suggestions I'm sure will do the trick. It's probably too late to see them in China, but here they are.

How about .... the Sumo Games? Everything Sumo. Just imagine the following events.

Sumo Synchronized Swimming. This could turn out to be the marquee event of the Olympics. Imagine seeing 400 and 500 pound athletes, upside down in the pool, kicking in perfect precision. It would be a true marriage of athleticism and pure artistry.

While we're in the pool, how about replacing the diving events with Sumo Cannonballs? The one who clears the most water out of the pool takes home the gold.

Moving on to the track, only the fastest Sumo will take center stage in the 10 meter dash. One hundred meters could prove hazardous to their health.

The Low Jump. The object will still be to propel one's body over the bar, just like the high jump, but I'm seeing winning heights more in the one to two foot range.

It would make sense that the Sumo with the best leaping ability would also compete on their nation's Sumo Basketball team. Let's drop the nets from ten feet to six to ensure we'll still see high flying dunks, although I doubt there will be many fast breaks.

Sumo Gymnastics would also be very entertaining, particularly the balance beam and floor exercises. Can you imagine the world's best Sumo doing double layouts and roundoffs? It would be incredible.

Sumo Dance, including ballet and the tango. Another event that's a must see.

Sumo Equestrian events. Because the riders will weigh a bit more than the horses are used to carrying, only the strongest and biggest horses need apply.

And how about a new event called Sumo Rodeo? Let's see how easily those bulls can toss a Sumo off their back.

Of course, you'd have to have Sumo wrestling itself. But why not add a few new twists with Team

Sumo and Cage Sumo? And how about Ultimate Fighting Sumo?

And finally, Sumo Eating. Let's see those athletes in training. What does it really take to get to that level? And here's a great idea for your advertisers. McDonalds, Burger King and the other fast food restaurants can add to their menus by offering customers the option to "Sumo Size" their portions.

They say you've got to dream big in life, and that's what the Sumo Games would be.

Respectfully yours,
Kevin S(umo) Engle

BABIES, CAR HORNS AND DOG HOUSES

Wes, my oldest nephew, called the other day and left a message. He said his wife Maya would be gaining weight over the next nine months. He seemed quite happy about it.

"That's strange. Why would he be happy she was about to pack on the pounds? I'll bet Maya's not thrilled."

A few days later, I got another weird call, this time from his dad, my brother John.

"You're going to be a great uncle!" he said. He was obviously excited.

Was I missing something? I already knew I was a great uncle. Rather awesome actually. Tell me something I don't know.

"What's the deal?" I asked my wife.

She could see I was confused, something she's used to.

"Wes and Maya are having a baby!"

"They are? Ohhhhhhhhhhhhhh. Why didn't they just say that?"

"They did. You just didn't catch it."

What can I say? Sometimes I'm a bit slow.

And speaking of slow, that's how I like to drive.

I was coming home from work one day last week when the guy behind me kept honking his horn. I figured he was testing it, checking to make sure it worked. It did. Quite well in fact. When he got the chance, he pulled up beside me and yelled.

"Take a hike buddy!" And then he sped off like a race car. He didn't seem to be in a good mood.

I was curious. How did he know I like to hike? Had he stuck around, I would've told him about our big trip later this year.

When I got home, I asked my wife about it.

"Geez," she said as she shook her head. "He wasn't telling you to go hiking."

"But that's what he said."

"He was mad that you were driving too slowly."

"He was? Ohhhhhhhhhhhhhhh. Why didn't he just say that?"

"He did."

How am I supposed to know what people mean, if they don't come out and say it? I'm not a mind reader.

But maybe I should be.

Just the other day my wife mentioned going on a diet to shed some holiday pounds.

"I'll bet you didn't gain more than five," I told her, trying to be encouraging.

"Kevin Engle! You're not supposed to agree with me when I say that."

"But, I was just, you said."

I give up.

And now, I'm in the dog house. Literally.

YOU ASKED

I've been getting tons of reader emails lately. At last count, I was up to seven. And that makes sense, considering how popular I've become from this column. People stop me everywhere to take photos, get my autograph, kiss a baby or two. You know how it is. Maybe not, but take my word for it. Anyway, because I'm so busy, I don't want to disappoint any of my fans by having to wait for an individual reply and thought this would be a great way to answer many of your most popular questions. Here goes.

Q: Judy from Warren County, VA asks "Is it true your wife writes all your columns?

A: That is absolutely NOT true. I can't believe someone would even suggest that. My wife (also named Judy by the way) only writes *some* of them. Mine are better though.

Q: HK from Pennsylvania wants to know "Why do you throw your mother-in-law "under the bus" so often? You're always making fun of her. I'll bet she's really nice."

A: I've never thrown my mother-in-law under the bus. As a matter of fact, I couldn't pick the woman up if I tried, let alone throw her anywhere. I just noticed that you two have the same initials, and you both live in Pennsylvania. How weird is that?

Q: Is it true you eat stink bugs? Bill from PETA
A: Yes I do, but only when there's nothing left in the fridge. It's an acquired taste. They're really not that bad once you get used to them. They're great for a snack and are low in cholesterol. I enjoy them in salad too.

Q: "Where do you get your article ideas?"
A: No doubt you've heard the expression "beg, borrow and steal". Next question?

Q: Do you really not know how to change tires on your car?
A: I barely know how to put gas in it. But I do know how to siphon from my neighbor's tank, something that's saved me a boat load of money over the years.

Q: Were you raised by wolves?
A: No, they were coyotes. Or maybe Siberian Huskies. I don't remember for sure, but I do like to have my belly rubbed.

Q: Sarah P from Alaska asks "Has Donald Trump talked to you about being his running mate?"
A: No comment. But I would like to say, as a man without hair, I admire any guy who can do what he does with what he's got on top. And Mr. Trump will be happy to know, should he ask, that I was born in the United States and have a copy of my birth certificate to prove it. Sarah, I have a question for you. Can you really see Russia from there?

Q: Barack O. from Washington, D.C. wants to know "Why didn't I see you at the Royal Wedding? I sat in my white house and watched the whole thing on TV. Were you there?"

A: Mr. O., the only Royals I know play baseball in Kansas City. Did one of their players get married?

Q: Are you and Charlie Sheen good friends?

A: I wouldn't say good friends. More like acquaintances. We've taken a few yoga classes together and go to the same psychiatrist.

Q: Brett from Green Bay, New York, Minneapolis and Mississippi says, "I'm recently retired and was hoping to watch a lot of football later this year. What do you think about the lockout in the National Football League? Are you upset about it?"

A: What I can't understand Brett is why somebody doesn't just call a locksmith. That's what I do when I get locked out. I can give them his number if they want it. He's available 24 hours a day and his prices are very reasonable.

And finally,

Q: KE says "I love your wit, your humor and your insight. I look forward to each of your columns. You're obviously very talented."

A: Thanks KE. I couldn't have said it better myself.

FINANCES, GIRLFRIENDS AND FAMILY TRIPS

I've been reading your column for several years, although I'm not sure why. Other than helping to pass the time while sitting on the pot, I don't like it all that much. And my wife thinks our pet pig is funnier than you. Anyway, I need some financial advice. I recently came in to some money. About $200 million, give or take, thanks to the lottery. My question is what do I do now?

One Lucky Dude

Dear Lucky Dude, what a coincidence. You read my column while "taking care of business". Guess where I write it? Congratulations on your winnings. Here's what I'd do. Give it away. All of it. And the sooner the better. You've heard the stories of lottery winners losing all their money and their life going down the toilet? Don't let that happen to you. Give me a call. I'll even do you a favor and take some of it off your hands.

P.S. I've heard pet pigs are very funny.

My girlfriend and I have been dating for almost two years. Lately, she's been dropping hints about taking our relationship to the next level. I wasn't ready to, but I really think she's the one. Should I let her pick it out or should I surprise her? What do you think? Oh yeah, she likes Chihuahuas. I like Great Danes.

Dog Gone It

> Dear Dog Gone It, heck if I know. But I'd spell everything out in the prenup.

My family has a problem. We can't agree on what to do for our summer vacation. The kids want to go to Disney. My husband mentioned the pyramids in Egypt. Me, I just want to sit on the beach and read a book. Can you help us?

Stressing over Summer

> Dear Stressing, this is an easy one. Go to the beach. Tell your kids when they can pay, they can say. Until then, they should be happy you'll take them anywhere. As for your husband, the Pyramids? Give me a break. He can see those on Google Earth. Why waste the time and money going there? And if you need a suggestion for a good book, check out one of my favorites. *The Best of Engle's Angle.*
>
> I love helping people.

■ ■ ■

The author grew up reading Dear Abby and Ann Landers. Obviously, it didn't help all that much.

S(NO)W MORE! PLEASE!

I give up. I can't take it anymore. All this snow is getting to me.

It all started a few days back when I was at the grocery store. You know, just me and 5,000 other crazies buying more milk and toilet paper that I didn't really need. Anyway, I turned the corner into the bread aisle when I saw it. The last loaf. I swear there was a golden halo shining all around it, like it was from heaven above. But I wasn't alone. Another shopper at the far end of the aisle spotted it at the same time. Our eyes met. It was on.

In a flash, I took off down the aisle, jumping over a little kid and pushing an old woman out of the way. We got there at the same instant. I went for the bread. She went for me, picking me up, twirling me around and flinging me to the floor. It was an epic battle, even if it only lasted three seconds. And the worst part? She got the bread. I got a headache. When I came to a few minutes later, with the store manager and a homeless guy standing over me, my head was throbbing. And that was a good day.

The next morning, I was shoveling, for the 17th time. After more than an hour of hard work, I finally cleared a four foot wall of snow from the end of the driveway. Two minutes later, the snow plow came by and blocked me in again. I swear I heard the driver laughing and taunting me as he drove past. I snapped. I threw down my shovel in disgust and chased after him, like a barking dog running behind a car. I did some barking of my own. "Get back here you #%*^@#$!!!" When I realized I wasn't going to catch him, I trudged back to my new wall of snow and shook my head in frustration. And then I smiled. He'd be back, and when he was, I'd be ready. Sure enough, thirty minutes later, when he returned, I hid behind my newly made wall of defense and pelted him with a few snow balls. He won't mess with me again.

As if the first snow wasn't enough, Mother Nature won't give up. She reached into her bag of tricks and threw more at me. I spent a few more hours yesterday snow blowing the driveway. Again.

This morning, when I looked outside, something didn't look right, although in the pre-dawn light, I couldn't tell what it was. A little while later, I knew. The wind had blown half the snow back onto the driveway. $%^^&#@!! Guess what I'll be doing this afternoon?

Between the woman at the grocery store, the snow plow driver and the wind, I give up! S(no)w more! Please!

PART SIX

That's Annoying

CUSTOMER SERVICE?

My day hasn't gotten off to the best start. The refrigerator is acting up. Again. I just had it fixed a month ago. Or so I thought. By 6AM, I'm back from the gas station, having bought five bags of ice to keep all of our food cold. By 6:30, I'm grilling the pork chops that were on tonight's menu. And that's when the fun continued. The following conversation actually occurred. I've altered the company's name slightly to protect the guilty.

> Kevin: Hi. My refrigerator isn't working. I'd like to schedule an appointment for someone to look at it.
> EARS: Sure thing. I need to ask you a few questions first. What's your name?
> K: Kevin Engle
> EARS: What state do you live in?
> K: Virginia.
> EARS: County?
> K: Warren.
> EARS: Coke or Pepsi?
> K: Huh?
> EARS: What do you like better?

K: I'm not sure. What does that have to do with my refrigerator?

EARS: Boxers or briefs, or none at all?

K: Excuse me?

EARS: Did you buy the refrigerator at one of our stores?

K: Yes, about four years ago.

EARS: Do you floss every day?

K: I try to, but what about my refrigerator?

EARS: We don't care how often your refrigerator flosses Mr. Engle. Social security number?

K: Why do you need that?

EARS: To access your credit report. Plus, we're nosy. How much money do you make?

K: You're kidding right?

EARS: No, I'm looking for a job. Democrat or Republican?

K: Independent.

EARS: Who are you going to vote for in the Presidential election?

K: Myself.

EARS: Do you believe in the Easter Bunny?

K: No, but I've seen Santa Claus.

EARS: Ok, I think I have enough information. I can have someone to your house in 10 days. What's better for you? 10PM-Midnight or 3AM-5AM?

K: Are you serious?

EARS: Yes sir. I take my job very seriously. Now what time would you like?

K: I don't think I can wait 10 days. My food won't last that long.

EARS: So what you're telling me Mr. Engle is now you don't want to schedule an appointment?
K: I guess I am.
EARS: I can't believe you just wasted my time. It's because of people like you that I'm looking for a new job. Is there anything else I can help you with today?
K: No thanks. You've done more than enough.
EARS: Would you like to apply for an EARS card?
K: I'll pass.
EARS: Thanks for calling EARS. Would you care to take a short survey about this call? There are only 100 questions.
K: Sure, I'd love to.

Our washing machine has been doing some weird things lately. Guess where we bought that?

Uh oh.

ONE FLOWER, TWO TOMATO PLANTS
AND A FREEZER FULL OF MEAT

15 Days Ago

My wife's big metal flower pot is full of blooming flowers. Pink, purple, yellow, white and orange. They're beautiful.

14 Days Ago

My wife's big metal flower pot has one lonely white bloom in it. Upon closer inspection, I see why. She's not going to be happy.

When she sees the damage, I cover my ears and head for safety.

"@#$$$^*&*##@!!! Dang deer! I'm gonna shoot'em!"

"They'll grow back," I tell her. "They did last year."

"We're gonna be eating deer steaks!"

"Now, now Judy. Calm down."

Last Sunday

"Look," my wife whispers as we sit on our back porch eating dinner. "She has three fawns again this year."

"That's three times in five years."

We silently watch as mom licks the salt block and her three little ones play.

Last Monday

I get home from work and walk around the house. When I pass by the garden, something catches my eye. When your entire garden consists of two tomato plants, that's not saying much.

What I notice is that one small green tomato lay on the ground. I look closer.

One of the plants looks different than it did the day before. A lot different. Where there had been oodles of green tomatoes yesterday, today there are none.

I cover my ears and scream. ""@#$$$^*&*##@!!! Dang deer! Judy's gonna shoot ya!"

Yesterday

I move the flower pots and tomato plants closer to the house, out of our furry foe's reach.

"They won't get them now," I tell her. "They won't walk on the concrete."

Today

"What the?"

Yup.

The pretty red begonias are no more.

"That's it!" my wife yells.

She mentions the name Phil and then storms off to the garage. Phil's my cousin. Several years ago, he was having similar problems. Phil's a smart guy. A scientist. Like any good scientist with a problem, he studied the situation. He considered various courses of action and then chose the one he thought was best.

One morning, after stepping out of the shower, and before he'd had a chance to put on any clothes, he eyed a hungry deer dining in his yard.

He opened a window.

"Bam!"

Problem solved.

We obviously have a problem. But never fear, my wife's a smart lady. She's a businesswoman. Like any good businesswoman with a problem, ...

■ ■ ■

The author recently purchased a new freezer. His wife said they'd be needing it.

IT'S SUPER. REALLY?

I was looking forward to watching both NFL Championship games on TV, although I'm not sure why. With everything on my screen, and in my ears, it's tough to actually follow the game. Or even see it.

First of all, I now know every conceivable statistic that relates to all four teams.

Were you aware that Baltimore's defense ranks best against the run whenever they're playing on the road, after 4PM, and in stadiums named after insurance companies?

Or that Tom Brady, New England's quarterback, has the highest passer rating in the league whenever he eats Cap'n Crunch® cereal the morning of a game in which the opponent's mascot is a lion, a tiger or some type of bird?

Or what about the San Francisco 49ers field goal kicker? He's never missed a kick at home that was less than 40 yards when he spent at least 35 bucks on gas and treated himself to a cherry Slurpee on his way to the game.

And the Giants allow fewer points against teams who wear yellow or purple jerseys. But only when they play them on the second Sunday of the month.

Got that?

And no matter how big your screen is, it's not big enough. The networks cram so much stuff on it, it's difficult to actually see the game. With just a quick glance, I know the score, the quarter, how much time remains, how many yards are needed for a first down and who's televising the game. And depending on the broadcaster, I see yellow, red and blue lines superimposed on the field, showing me the line of scrimmage as well as the first down marker. I'm surprised they don't have a moving colored line whenever the quarterback throws the ball.

During the regular season, there's even more, like the updated score of every game in the world, including that all important cricket match in India and the rugby final in New Zealand. It's a wonder I can sleep at night after seeing so many things flash on my screen. If I want pop up ads, I can get those online.

And what about the endless self promotions?

On Fox, it's "In case you didn't catch it the first thirty times we said it, *American Idol* will be on tonight after the game."

And over at CBS, "*60 Minutes* will be shown in its entirety after the broadcast, except on the West coast. And don't forget about the Masters. You know, that golf tournament that takes place **three months** from now? We'll have that too."

Give me a break.

Baseball's not any better. They even have a small infield in the corner of the screen. A filled in diamond means there's a runner on that base. You have to be an expert in symbols to decipher it all. And while I'm staring at that stuff, trying to crack the code, I'm missing the game itself. And when I do watch, I see a different ad behind home plate with every pitch.

Here's a suggestion for all the networks.

Can I just watch the game?

That would be nice, but I'm not counting on it.

If I can stay awake long enough to see the Super Bowl, after about 25 hours of pregame coverage, I'll get more of the same. Statistics that make me scratch my head, a screen full of graphics, and 8000 promos for all of NBC's new shows.

No wonder why everyone likes the Super Bowl commercials.

MONKEYS, BANANAS AND BEARS. OH MY!

"Make lots of noise. And stay together."

I could feel the sweat trickling down my back. This was serious stuff. There really were bears out there, and I could be their next dinner.

Maybe this hiking trip wasn't such a good idea.

"If you see one," the ranger went on, "don't move!"

"What if I faint?" I asked her jokingly.

She failed to see the humor. "I wouldn't do that," she replied without cracking a smile or missing a beat. "Don't make any sudden movements. Ninety-nine per cent of the time, they won't bother you."

I was now very concerned about that other one per cent.

My wife and I and a cousin were on vacation in Glacier National Park. Before heading out for our first big hike, we stopped at the ranger station for information. What we got was the crap scared out of us. Park Ranger Susie Sunshine had all kind of good things to share.

"If a bear runs toward you," she went on, "hold your ground. Most of the time, they're only bluffing."

Most of the time? Only bluffing? Was I playing poker with a bear? I'm not very good at poker with people.

The woman was relentless.

"If somehow you get between a momma and her cubs, *that's* when you need to be concerned."

I guess she didn't notice that I was hyperventilating. I already was concerned. And I was still inside the building. After talking to her, I wasn't sure we'd make it safely back to the car.

"What about bear spray?" my wife asked. "Should we get some?"

"I would. I always carry it. Even in the house. And it's most effective when your target is very close."

This lady was a comedian, but now it was me who wasn't laughing at the jokes. If a bear gets that close to me, I'll be doing one of two things. Running faster than any human being ever has, or scrambling up a tree like a monkey after the last banana.

She went on for a few more minutes, telling us what to do, and not do, if we crossed paths with a grizzly. I didn't catch any of it. I was too busy scribbling my last will and testament on a trail map.

At some point my wife told her "Thanks" and then pushed me toward the door.

"Have a good time," Ranger Sunshine told us. "And don't forget about the cougars."

Cougars?

We'd been planning this trip for more than a year and now, after 15 minutes with Susie Sunshine, I was ready to catch the first plane home. I had no desire to be served up as a delicacy for Mr. Bear.

I stumbled out the door and headed straight for the car.

"Now what?" I asked, hoping either my wife or cousin would say the word 'airport'.

"We'll be fine," my wife said. "We just need to be careful and stay together."

Not exactly what I was hoping to hear.

"I know where I'm going," I told her.

"Where?"

"Back to the room. I'll be hiding under the bed."

ALL I WANTED TO KNOW

"If you'd like to pay off your loan, press 22. If you'd like to refinance, press 23. If you'd like the main menu, press 99."

"Customer service," I said through clenched teeth, annoyed and frustrated that I'd been listening to these ##$%%@# voice prompts for the past five minutes and was still no closer to where I wanted to be.

All I wanted to know was when my new payment booklet would be in the mail.

"I'm sorry. I don't understand that request. Let's start over. If you'd like to"

I couldn't take it anymore. "Customer service!" I yelled, ready to fight this stupid answering system.

"Please hold while your call is transferred."

"Finally," I said as sweat poured down my face and arms. When I get agitated, I sweat. I was agitated.

According to the letter I received last week, my mortgage was being transferred from one of the bank's subsidiaries to another. It was almost time for my next payment and I thought the new coupon booklet would be here by now.

"Hi, I'm Ms. Randolph," came the cheery voice on the other end of the phone, "how can I help you?"

"Thank goodness. A real human being," I muttered. "All I want to know is when I'll receive my new payment book in the mail. That's it."

"Sure, I can help you with that. Let me get some information first."

After giving her my address, phone number, account number, blood type, what I was buying my wife for Christmas and the secret ingredients to Coca Cola, she found what she needed.

"I see your wife is the primary account holder. May I speak with her?"

The question struck fear in my heart. I knew where this conversation was going.

"No, she's not here."

Maybe, just maybe, she'd still answer my question. After all, all I wanted to know was when my payment book would arrive.

"I'm sorry Mr. Engle, but I can't discuss the account with you."

"Rrrrrrrrrrrrrrrrrrr!"

My hopes for success were quickly extinguished, like a fire hose dousing a candle. There wasn't a chance in hell Ms. Randolph was going to tell me anything.

But I pleaded my case anyway.

"Doesn't it count that I'm the one who signs the check every month?"

"We appreciate that very much Mr. Engle, but because of privacy concerns, I'm not allowed to discuss this account with anyone but Mrs. Engle."

Twenty-one minutes and thirty-nine seconds after dialing, I hung up in disgust, still without an answer to my simple question. And all I wanted to know ...

Oh screw it.

THAT WAS NO LADY

My wife and I are standing in line to rent skis.

There are four lines of skiers and four employees helping everyone.

The couple in front of us are trying on helmets and it's taking a little longer than I'd like.

I'm impatient, as usual. I want to get my stuff and get on the mountain. I want to ski, not stand here in line.

They pick their helmets and head for the next station. Boots.

It's our turn.

That is, until we hesitate for a split second and the lady and her son to our left cut in front of us.

The steam shoots out of my ears instantaneously.

If there's one thing that ticks me off, it's when people cut in front of me.

Actually, there are a lot of things that tick me off, but line cutting, ooooh, that's near the top of the list.

The little boy glanced back at us a couple times, as if he knew Mommy had done a bad thing.

That's right sonny, your mommy is a bad person. She's a line cutter.

"Calm down," my wife said. "We're here to have fun."

She was right. We were there to have fun.

But at that moment, I wasn't, and she knew it.

Not even the words of the famous philosopher, Frank Costanza, from the TV show *Seinfeld*, calmed me down.

"Serenity now!!!"

No, my blood pressure was in the red zone and climbing.

When the line cutter and her son headed off to get their boots, I did exactly what my wife didn't want me to.

Say something.

"Thanks for cutting in front of us."

She mumbled something, but I didn't listen. I couldn't hear her anyway. The adrenaline was flowing and my heart was pounding too loudly in my chest to hear anything.

My wife has cautioned me on more than one occasion about saying anything in situations like this.

"You never know what someone might do."

And she's right.

How could I be sure this woman wasn't a professional cage fighter who'd immediately slam me to the ground? Talk about embarrassing.

I couldn't be sure, and that's exactly why I should keep my mouth shut.

But I can't.

Line cutters infuriate me. I had to vent. For my blood pressure's sake.

And besides, I'd eaten my Wheaties® for breakfast. I was feeling confident.

I knew I could handle the kid and my wife could take care of the mom, cage fighter or not.

After all, gentlemen are supposed to treat ladies with respect.

But that was no lady.

WAKE ME WHEN IT'S OVER

Do you love elections as much as I do? Hearing the same radio ads for weeks and seeing the same TV commercials a thousand times? It's great isn't it? Those 30 and 60 second spots that make you feel all warm and fuzzy inside as the candidates trash and bash each other?

If the truth be told, which sometimes doesn't happen during campaigns, my favorite part of the election process is when it's over. My wife has had to stop me on more than one occasion from tossing our TV out the window after seeing the same ad three times within thirty minutes. Is it too much to ask the candidates to get along? Yeah, I know it is, but you can dream right? This is America. A land of dreamers. And speaking of dreams, I had one the other night. I was watching a debate between the two Presidential candidates. It went something like this.

> Donald T: "My opponent is truly deserving to win this election. She has an outstanding record, always acts in the best interests of her constituents and is a genuinely nice person."
>
> Hillary C: "Oh Donald, you're too kind. Don't sell yourself short. You too would make a great

President. You have the experience, the ability to get things done and you love puppies. In fact, I'll probably vote for you myself."

DT: "Aw shucks, Hillary. That's very nice of you. But I hear you've got three dogs at your house and a couple of cats as well."

HC: "Actually Don, it's four dogs. But don't forget to tell everyone you once saved a deer that was hit by a car. You're truly a compassionate human being."

DT: "That's true, but didn't you want to be a nurse? Nurses care about people, and that's why you'd do a bang up job for this great country."

HC: "Yeah, I did, but I know for a fact you coached your daughter's soccer team and your sons' Little League baseball squads, so you're concerned about our nation's youth. That's important. And didn't you organize a neighborhood crime watch program?"

DT: "Yes, but my sources also tell me that you and your family volunteer at a food bank once a month. Service to others is important to you. That's just another reason why I am personally endorsing you for this election."

HC: "Donald, if I am fortunate enough to win, I'd like you to play a key role in helping me get things done for this country. With your contacts and negotiating skills, we could accomplish some great things."

DT: "And if I'm elected, I'm going to appoint you to a special task force to help solve our nation's toughest problems. I have the utmost confidence in your abilities to cut through the red tape and do what needs to be done."

HC: "Are you and your wife free after the debate? My husband and I would like to have dinner with you. I have some other ideas that I'd like to discuss."

DT: "Sure thing, but only if you'll let me pay. I like your husband a lot."

HC: "You got a deal. Do you guys like Mexican? Taco Bell is having a two-for-one special on burritos."

I can't wait until the next election. I just know it's going to be positive, uplifting and good for the country.

Did I mention that I can't wait until the next election? It's going to be positive, uplifting and good for the country.

And in conclusion, I'd just like to say that I can't wait until the next election. It's going to be positive, uplifting and good for the country.

CLICK

I've just about had it with the phone. Here's why.

"Hello?"

"Mr. Engle?"

"Yes."

"Hi, my name is Joe and I'm calling from the local chapter of the Democratic National Party."

"Ok."

"Would you like to make a donation for the next Presidential campaign?"

"You're kidding right? We just had an election."

"No sir. I'm quite serious. If you donate $100, you'll become a distinguished Donkey club member."

"Didn't President Obama have tons of money left over from his campaign?"

"Yes he did, but we want more."

Click.

"Hello?"

"Mr. Engle?"

"Yes."

"Hi, I'm Amber, a junior at Duke University. How are you this evening?"

"Fantastic. How are you?"

"Fine, thanks. I'm calling to thank you for your donation to last year's Annual Fund and to see how much you'd like to contribute this year. If you give $100, you'll become a member of the bodacious Blue Devil bunch."

"Amber, I don't mean to be rude, but I had asked that no one call me until June. I donate every year and that's when I make my contribution."

"We don't want you to forget."

"How could I? Someone calls me every week."

Click.

"Hello?"

"Is this Jesus?"

"Excuse me?"

"Are you Jesus?"

"No."

"Are you sure?"

"Very."

"I'm Bill from Visa, and Jesus owes us money. This is the number he gave us."

"Bill, I'm sorry to disappoint you, but I've had this number for close to five years, and Jesus hasn't lived here in that time."

"You wouldn't be lying to me, would you?"

Click.

"Hello?"

"Hi, this is Chad from the Yellow Pages. I'd like to talk with you about your business listing, Doggy Do Do."

"Chad, sorry to tell you this, but I don't have a business."

"Really? You wouldn't be lying to me, would you?"

Click.

"Hello?"

"Mr. Engle?"

"He doesn't live here anymore."

"You wouldn't be lying to me, would you?"

"As a matter of fact, yes I would."

Click.

"SURVEY SAYS!"

Monday morning. I take my car to the shop to get the oil changed.

Tuesday afternoon. They send me an email.

"We'd love your feedback," they tell me. "Please click this link to take a short survey."

My wife goes out of town on a business trip.

When she gets back, she receives a message from the airline and one from the hotel.

Two more surveys.

I call my credit card company to ask them a simple question about our account.

A few days later, you guessed it, another email.

Another customer satisfaction survey.

I log on to my bank's website to get my monthly statement. Before I can, a message pops up on my screen.

"Would I rate my online experience?"

I call AAA to ask them something and before I can speak to an agent, this is what I hear.

"Press 1 to stay on the line after the call to answer a few questions. Press 2 for no."

Enough with the dang surveys!

You know what would really make me a satisfied customer? Don't ask me to take one!

Not unless you give me something for it. And hey, I'm easy. It doesn't have to be much. I'll take anything.

Sure, a $1000 Walmart or Lowe's gift card sounds great, but they only give you *a chance* to win one. And what's *the chance* of that happening?

I think we all know the answer to that question.

If you want me to take your survey, I want something in return. A guarantee.

I always complete the one for Panda Express. Why? A free entrée on my next visit.

And at Subway, who wouldn't want a free cookie?

Are you getting the hint? Bribe me.

My wife loves those rocking chairs from Cracker Barrel. And she'll have one, as soon as I pay for it with my credit card. Not because I told them my eggs were runny, the bacon was too crisp, but the service was great.

The Service Manager at the garage even tells me how to answer the questions.

"We'd appreciate all 5's," he says. "Anything less and we get a failing grade."

Really? You should've thought about that when you were 45 minutes late starting the work on my car.

If I get take out from a fast food restaurant and you give me what I ordered, it tastes good and I didn't have to pay too much for it, I'm satisfied.

"Is there a reason you weren't highly satisfied?"

I don't know!

And no, I didn't experience any problems during my visit, although the bathroom could've been cleaner.

If I answered every survey request I received, I wouldn't have time to get my free cookie.

And if that happened, I'd be highly unsatisfied. And you can be sure I wouldn't recommend your business to a friend because of it.

What can I say?

I love chocolate chip cookies.

Especially free ones.

■ ■ ■

The author used to watch *The Match Game* when Richard Dawson was the host. "Survey says!"

NOT TODAY!

"Do you need help with something?"

It's always nice when someone wants to help you, but this guy knew I didn't need help. He knew exactly why I was there and exactly what I was doing.

"No thanks," I said as I continued pressing buttons on the remote. Not unless he knew what channel CNBC was on.

"Just waiting for your car?"

Who says there are no stupid questions? Of course I'm waiting for my car. Do people wait in these little rooms at car dealerships, the ones with the uncomfortable chairs and 25 different magazines scattered about, for some other reason?

"Yup."

I wasn't trying to be rude, but I didn't want to talk to this guy. I knew where this was going. Someplace I didn't want to go. This was just his way of starting the conversation. The one I didn't want to have. What he was really asking, without saying the words, was "how would you like to buy a new car today?"

"What do you drive?"

Here we go. I could feel the knot tighten in the back of my neck. I clenched my jaw.

"A Ford Escape."

I should've lied. Told him my license was suspended.

"Do you like it?"

This is exactly why I despise car dealerships. The second you get there, you're in their cross hairs. You're a piece of meat. An injured gazelle on the African savannah, being circled by a pride of hungry lions. It's only a matter of time before they pounce.

"I do."

We made eye contact for the first time. He knew I didn't want to have this conversation, but he kept going anyway.

"What year is it?"

"I'm here for a state inspection man, not to buy a new car. Will you leave me alone?"

That's what I wanted to say.

'2006' is what I did say.

Before he could ask me his next question, 'how many miles did I have on it?', and then the inevitable 'don't you think it's time for a new one?', the service manager miraculously appeared from around the corner, or maybe it was heaven, and said those magic words.

"Your car is ready Mr. Engle."

"Praise Jesus!" I cried out as I knelt down and kissed the dirty floor.

And just like that, the conversation was over. He walked away, defeated, but no doubt in search of his next target. I quickly put down the remote and followed the service manager to his desk. I'd survived. All I had to do now was pay the bill and get out.

Who teaches car salesman to be like this? Do they learn this stuff their first day on the job? I realize they're trying to earn a living, but come on!

Can you imagine walking on to the lot and no one approaching you? That'd be great. I'd love it.

The next time I am shopping for a new car, in about fifteen or twenty years, I'm going to wear a big sign that says "Just looking. Don't bother me."

I bet they will anyway.

EVERY GROUNDHOG HAS HIS DAY (AND IT'S NOT ALWAYS IN FEBRUARY)

Marmot. Woodchuck. Groundhog.

Whatever you call them, we have them.

And they're not welcome here.

They're getting into my wife's flowers. Eating them, smashing them, and breaking them.

I'm sure the groundhogs are happy. I know my wife is not.

This weekend, I spotted a sizeable hole in our backyard. I'd never seen one that deep. I thought it was a sinkhole.

My wife informed me otherwise.

"Damn groundhogs!" she yelled.

She's upset.

She wants to do something about them. As a kid, my wife hunted with her dad and brothers. Ok, I think you know where I'm going with this. I wasn't too excited about that idea and suggested we pursue an alternate route. Something a bit more animal-friendly.

We have a cage. The kind to catch animals. If she can't kill groundhogs, my wife wants to catch groundhogs.

I've seen those beasts, and let me tell ya, unless they start on Nutrisystem® or Slim-Fast!® real soon, they ain't gonna fit in that cage. My wife thinks otherwise.

Ok, let's assume she's right. Even if those groundhogs can squeeze their fat pudgy bodies into that cage, then what?

We don't own a pick-up truck. Our cars don't have a trunk. I have no intention of transporting a live groundhog in the back of my car. Not while I'm behind the wheel. What if Mr. or Mrs. Groundhog busts out of that cage? Talk about distracted driving.

The last time I was in the wildlife relocation business, the target was squirrels and we had a trunk. I felt reasonably confident I could accomplish the task without incurring any injuries to myself or damage to the car.

I don't have that same level of confidence this time.

"Don't be a baby!" my wife said.

There are times in life when you can shame someone into doing something they don't want to do. Make them feel guilty enough that they'll cave. This isn't one of those times. There is absolutely nothing my wife can say or do to change my mind. I will not relocate groundhogs in the back of my car. And I'm not about to let her do it either.

I love my wife. Very much.

If that groundhog got out of the cage and she wrecked our car because of it, I'd never forgive myself.

It's paid for.

MY THIRD FAVORITE

What's your favorite day of the year?

I have two. My birthday and Christmas.

My third favorite is right around the corner. The exact date changes, but it's always on a Wednesday. This year it's on the 7th. Of November.

What's so special about that day?

It's the day *AFTER* the Presidential election.

Brothers and sisters, can you say "Amen"?

If I can survive until then, I will have made it through another Presidential election. And when I lay my head on my pillow after the polls close, I'll do so with a smile on my face.

Why?

Because my life, and yours, are about to get a lot better, and it has nothing to do with who won. Beginning on November 7th, we won't have to put up with the following:

No more political surveys and other calls urging us to vote for one of the candidates.

No more oversized ads in our mailbox telling us why one candidate would do a great job as President, while the other is no better than a heaping pile of rotting garbage.

No more TV ads like these:

> Commercial #1 –President Obama has done a great job leading our country.
> Commercial #2 – President Obama has done a horrible job leading our country.
> Commercial #3 – Mitt Romney cares deeply about the middle class.
> Commercial #4 – Mitt Romney couldn't care less about the middle class.
> Commercial #5 – Vote "yes" for Question #7 on the Maryland ballot.
> Commercial #6 – Vote "no" for Question #7 on the Maryland ballot.

(Hey Maryland, I live in Virginia. If I voted 'yes' or 'no' for Question #7, I'd get arrested for voter fraud. On second thought, it might be worth going to jail. At least I wouldn't have to suffer through any more of your commercials.)

No more annoying radio ads for the Senate race in Virginia. I keep hearing the same one at least thirty-five times an hour, and it's a stupid ad to begin with. Every time it comes on, I turn down the volume.

No more debates. You know, those televised events where the candidates exceed their time limit, don't answer the question, talk about what they want to, and say bad stuff about the other guy? And no more dissecting the debate for days afterward telling me who won.

And finally, no more polls from *The Wall Street Journal*, the *Washington Post*, the *New York Times*, ABC, CBS, NBC, CNN and the Disney Channel informing me about everything imaginable, including who kids would most like to play with at the White House, the First Dog Bo or Mrs. Romney's horse.

As far as I'm concerned, my third favorite day of the year can't get here soon enough.

And I'll tell you something else. Things are going to be different the next time. I'm running for President in four years. And here's why you should vote for me.

I'll work hard to strengthen Social Security, lower the unemployment rate, improve our schools, eliminate the debt and insure everyone has affordable quality health care. My administration will also partner with industry to develop renewable energy sources and we'll work tirelessly for world peace.

Sound familiar?

Some things never change.

And that's why the day after Election Day will always be my third favorite day of the year.

■ ■ ■

My name is Kevin Engle and I approved this article.

EASY? I WISH.

Remember the Easy Button™ from those Staples® commercials? Press it and the voice says "That was easy".

I like easy. But these days, what you think should be easy is anything but.

Background information and legal disclaimer: What you are about to read is true. I have changed the names. Not to protect the innocent, but me. I don't want to get sued.

My wife and I have a credit card with U.S. Speedy (name changed). I recently spoke with one of their customer service reps. I'll call her Joy (name changed).

Here's what happened.

"Hello Mr. Engle, my name is Joy. How may I help you today?" She sounded like she'd overdosed on happy pills. I'm all for liking your job, but Joy was waaaaaaaaaaay over the top. I was suspicious. No one is that happy, especially at work.

I explained to her there was a $10.93 finance charge on my account that shouldn't be there.

"Yes, I see your annual account fee was waived. But because you didn't pay it, a finance charge was assessed," she cheerfully explained, as if it were a good thing.

"I don't understand. If I didn't owe the annual fee, why would you assess finance charges against it?"

"That's just how we do it here at U.S. Speedy. How do you think we make so much money? What you should have done Mr. Engle is pay the annual fee and then asked to be reimbursed. Then you wouldn't have been assessed the finance charge."

"But no one told me that. And I'd like it taken off my bill."

"Oh, I see," she said a bit less joyfully. "May I put you on hold?"

What choice did I have?

Two minutes later, she returned. "Mr. Engle, I was able to credit your account for half of the finance charge, but I can't eliminate the other half. But there's a silver lining to all of this. I'm going to give you bonus miles."

Joy was happy again. Mr. Engle wasn't.

"So you still want me to pay some of the finance charge?"

"Yes, that's the best I can do."

I asked her to try again.

"May I put you on hold again?" Her happy pills were starting to wear off.

Two minutes later, Joy was back. "I'm sorry Mr. Engle, there's nothing more I can do. I've already gone out on a limb for you by crediting your account for half of the amount and giving you those bonus miles."

Silence.

Joy knew what I was thinking, and they weren't happy thoughts.

"That was a poor choice of words on my part Mr. Engle. Let's just say I did everything I could for you."

I did the only thing I could. The same thing everyone does in these situations. "May I speak with your manager?"

"Yes, but she won't be able to help you any more than I can."

"Ok, but I'd still like to talk with her." All the joy was gone, and so was she when her supervisor got on the line.

The supervisor put me on hold, did her thing and then told me what I wanted to hear before I ever picked up the phone.

"Alright Mr. Engle, I've eliminated the entire finance charge and you'll receive those bonus miles for your troubles."

"Thanks," I muttered as I hung up, a little more dazed and confused than I normally am. Wasn't that a great way to spend 21 minutes and 37 seconds of my day? All to fix something that should've been easy.

I needed some stress relief. I pressed the Easy Button™ on my desk.

Nothing.

I pressed it again.

Still nothing.

Dead battery.

Go figure.

ENOUGH ALREADY!

The phone rings.

"Private Caller".

We keep getting these calls.

And I keep ignoring them.

"If you answer it," my wife says, "maybe they won't call back."

"I'm not so sure about that."

I pick it up anyway.

"Hello."

It's a recording.

"If you'd like to lower the interest rate on your credit card, please press 1. This is your final chance to take advantage of this special offer."

I hang up.

I'm not interested in lowering the interest rate on my credit card.

And even if I was, I seriously doubt that was my last chance to do so. I'd bet the limit on all my credit cards they'll call again in a few days.

We got a post card last week.

"THIS IS YOUR FINAL NOTICE" it said in large red letters.

And other nice things, like "Deadline", "Please Respond Within 5 Business Days", "Your Immediate Attention is Required", and my favorite, "This is our FINAL attempt to contact you, after this attempt, this offer will expire."

Really? I hope so. My nine year old car's warranty expired thousands of miles ago. Quit bugging me about it ok? I'm not interested in your extended warranty plan. And who are you anyway? Are you even a legitimate company?

Stop it!

You've been sending me these dang post cards for the last five years and I'll bet you'll send me another one in a few months.

Enough already!

A few months back I bought a DVD from a company that sells educational products.

I learned one thing for sure.

That was a mistake.

Sure, I picked up some tips on how to take better photographs while on vacation, but as soon as the DVD arrived, so did the barrage of emails. And catalogs.

They've been relentless.

I quickly got tired of the emails and unsubscribed from their list. The latest thirtysomething page catalog that just came says "WE WANT YOU BACK!"

It's nice to be wanted, but I'm not ready to come back. In fact, I may never be. Not if this keeps up.

I made a few small donations to several charities recently.

That was a mistake too.

Guess who's now sending me lots of emails and stuff in the mail asking for more money? I wanted them to use my donation to do something good, not to send me stuff in the mail.

And now we're getting things from other similar charities I've never heard of before.

I just shake my head.
The phone rings.
It's a Pennsylvania number.
I recognize it.
It's my mother-in-law.
I let it ring.
She'll call back.

■ ■ ■

The author called about the extended warranty plan. He told them he's not interested. He's going to call tomorrow and tell them again. And the day after that as well. Two can play this game.

"DUE TO CIRCUMSTANCES BEYOND OUR CONTROL, ..."

"Due to circumstances beyond our control, we are unable to take your call at this time. Please try again later."

If I hear that message one more time, I'm gonna jump through this phone. But it's my fault. If I would've changed my email password like I was supposed to, I wouldn't be listening to this recording for the fifth day in a row.

I have two email accounts at work, one for my employer and one for our customer. I use the customer email account all the time. I hardly ever check my company's email. Once a week. Maybe. The only messages I get from my company are the ones telling me what our new vision statement is.

Typically, when it's time to reset your password, even if it's expired, you type the old one and then the new one twice. My employer doesn't do it that way. If you don't change it every sixty days, you're locked out. No warning. No nothing. End of story. At that point, you have one option. Call the Computer (No) Help desk. If you can actually talk to a human being, it's no big deal. They do their thing and I'm reading the company's new vision statement a minute later.

So I called. And waited. And waited more. I had to leave a message.

"I need to reset my password. I'm here until 2:00 today. My number is

xxx-xxI-diot."

When I came in the next morning, someone had actually returned my call with a ticket number. Ok, we're making progress.

I called again. And that's when I heard my favorite recording for the first time.

"Due to circumstances beyond our control, we are unable to take your call at this time. Please try again later."

Huh? Circumstances beyond their control? What the heck does that mean? Do I really want to know?

I tried again the next day. Same thing.

And the next. Same thing.

This went on for more than a week. At first, I didn't mind. But as it dragged on, the ridiculousness of the situation started to annoy me.

And then one morning when I got in, there was a voice mail from the day before.

"This is Luke. I'm calling to see if you've gotten your issue resolved. If not, please call 1-800-No-Help!"

I had to laugh.

I tried again.

"Due to circumstances beyond our control, ..."

I checked with my Team Lead.

"You just have to keep trying," he told me. "Sorry."

And then, out of the blue, my phone rang. It was Luke.

"Have you gotten your password reset?"

"No," I told him as the tears ran down my face, happy that I was actually talking to someone who could help me.

"Ok," he said ten seconds later, "I've reset it to You're1BigIdiot."

"Thanks."

After lunch, I accessed my email for the first time in almost three weeks. After deleting the message about our company's new vision statement, I typed in the temporary password and then my new one.

I hit "Enter".

"Your password does not meet the minimum security requirements."

"What?"

I stared at the message for a minute, confused. My new password was the same length as the old one, and a mix of numbers, letters and special characters, just as before.

And then I did what any intelligent person would do in that situation. I retyped the exact same thing.

"Your password does not meet the minimum security requirements."

I shook my head.

One more try. Same error message.

I picked up the phone and dialed.

"Due to circumstances beyond our control, ..."

I give up.

FROM LOG HOUSE TO TREE HOUSE

My wife and I live in a log house. We like our house.

The birds do too. They want to make it theirs as well.

They've been building nests on it all spring.

After removing about 50 from the same spot, I gave up. I told my wife I didn't want to knock another one down and see an egg in it.

And now, another bird is at it again in a different location.

We've been doing battle several times a day.

Using my fully-extended golf ball retriever, I carefully remove the newest dirt and moss nest from above a spotlight. Thirty minutes later, my nemesis, undeterred, is at it again.

The wood bees like my house.

And why wouldn't they? It's made of wood.

We've had to resort to the professionals to deal with them.

And last week, the carpenter ants decided to stop by.

I wasn't in the mood for company. If they would've called ahead of time, maybe, but they just dropped in without letting us know.

They keep coming to the same spot. One corner of the garage. Yesterday we found out why. A dead toad.

We got rid of him but they don't know that yet.

The woodpeckers like my house, although they've been keeping their distance lately thanks to an annoyingly loud squawk box we put on the front porch. It emits woodpecker distress sounds from sun up to sundown. It's 6:00 in the morning and it just started for the day. I'm sure my neighbors love me.

I wouldn't be surprised if we soon get another visitor. The police, telling me to turn the dang thing off.

A few weeks ago we'd just gone to bed and were half asleep when we heard something in the attic directly above us. A scratching sound.

A squirrel?

Great.

We screamed and beat on the walls for an hour. I even turned on the decibel-blasting smoke alarm a few times.

A week later, when the ringing in my ears had subsided, the scratching returned.

A guy came and closed off two small holes where we think the beast was getting in. And we decided that squirrel was actually a mouse.

My lawn isn't the greatest, but the voles don't care. Last year it was the moles. It was so bad we paid someone to fight them, although the moles still came out on top. This spring, my yard looks like it was bombed. There are little vole holes all over the place. And now, another as yet unidentified creature is making bigger holes going after the voles.

I think we have a groundhog too.

A guy I used to work with said I lived in the woods.

He was right.

The animals certainly think so.

They're trying to take over the place.

Not if I can help it.

I spend a good chunk of my day, too much of it, being the angry landlord, evicting squatters and trying to exterminate others.

It's exhausting.

And I need a nap.

But I can't right now.

My bird friend is back.

■ ■ ■

The author is moving. To a tree house in the woods. Let's see how the animals like that. Two can play this game.

THE BIG BAD BIN AND THE
YELLOW DVD

My wife and I were in Walmart the other day. And believe me, it wasn't my idea.

We'd been in the car six hours and were almost home.

But no, we had to make a detour.

Right now.

My wife was having coworkers to the house in a few days for an all day meeting. She wanted to get a DVD as a gift.

"I could do it tomorrow," I told her.

"You already have enough to do," she said.

I did, but at this very moment, shopping at Walmart tomorrow sounded a lot better than shopping at Walmart today. And besides, we were just at another Walmart two days ago getting stuff for this meeting. Why couldn't we have thought of it then?

But here we were. Fifteen minutes from home, but oh so far away.

Have you seen those large circular bins in Walmart? The ones that hold 10,000 movies, all for five bucks?

That's where we were.

I'd come across the yellow DVD in one of these bins a few months back. I was just looking to see what was there when I found it. We had seen the movie before and liked it. It was worth five bucks.

But today was different.

Today, we weren't just looking to see what was in the bin. We were looking for the yellow DVD. The needle in the haystack.

Maybe we'd get lucky and find it right away.

Yeah, and maybe I like cuddling up with grizzly bears.

"Ok," I said as we exited off the Interstate. "If we're doing this, we're using a shopping cart to make it easier."

I underestimated. We could've used four shopping carts, although we settled for one.

I grabbed and tossed, barely reading the titles. All I cared about were yellow DVDs. And I found them, just not the one we were after.

"Look," my wife said somewhat enthusiastically as she dug up other movies we liked.

"That's nice," I said as I kept grabbing and tossing into the cart, getting more impatient with each handful.

And then I had a brainstorm.

"Ask an employee if they even have it in stock. They can check their inventory system."

I'd hate to think we were doing this for nothing.

She asked, but didn't get a definitive answer. I tried a few minutes later and didn't fare any better.

We kept looking, even after we'd filled up the cart. Now, we were looking and throwing back all at the same time, no doubt seeing the same movies the other had already checked out thirty seconds before.

I wanted to quit. I wanted to return the 879 DVDs piled high in our shopping cart and go home. But not so fast. After all, we had another bin to go through.

Yeah, a second bin.

"Excuse me," said a guy in broken English, "can you tell me where" some department was.

I knew that was going to happen.

"I'm sorry," I told him as I kept tossing DVDs, "I don't work here."

This was like playing slots in Vegas. You just knew if you quit now, the jackpot would be the next one, the one you didn't play.

After forty minutes of this, I didn't really care.

And no, we didn't find the yellow DVD in bin #2 either.

But we did spend 20 bucks on four other movies.

■ ■ ■

The Manager told us we could order it on line for $4.50. I wish I'd known that forty minutes ago. %##$%^&***!!!

PART SEVEN

Memories

DOES HE REALLY KNOW BEST?

With Father's Day just around the corner, I started thinking about all the stuff my dad taught me growing up. Sure he showed me how to pick up women and hot wire a car, but whose dad doesn't teach his son those things? Here are five of the most important lessons I learned from my father.

Story #1 – Dad grew up on a farm. As a young freckled-faced red head, he was a bit on the ornery side. Years later, he still is. One summer day, he came across some young ladies sun bathing. He didn't like it all that much that they could relax while he had chores to do in the hot sun. Every problem needs a solution. His solution? Shower them with cow manure. For some reason, they didn't take kindly to it.

Lesson #1 – Treat the ladies well. Don't give them crap.

Story #2 – Late October. I'm about seven years old. One night my brother and I were going through the neighborhood with some friends throwing field corn at windows. That's what you did to scare people at Halloween. As we got close to home, my dad, all 6' 2", 250 pounds of him, jumped out of the bushes. Wearing a white sheet and looking like a very large ghost, he screamed bloody murder. We all scattered. All but the one neighbor kid who was too scared to move and passed out right in front of him.

Lesson #2 – You can never have too much personal liability insurance.

Story #3 – My mother was in the hospital for a few days. Dad got home from work and started making supper for his two hungry sons. He never had a lot of training in the kitchen. When my brother saw what was on the menu, Eggo® waffles, he wasn't all that impressed. He told my dad he wasn't impressed and wasn't about to eat them. And he didn't. That was fine with me. I loved Eggo® waffles. I ate mine and some of his.

Lesson #3 – Waffles aren't just for breakfast anymore.

Story #4 – My dad drove a lot for his job. One day, he was in Ohio on his way to a construction site. He got stopped for speeding. Later that night, coming home, he got stopped again. By the same cop.

Lesson #4 – If you're going to fly, do it in a plane.

Story #5 – We're on the golf course. Dad hits an errant tee shot into the woods. A minute later, we hear a thunderous roar from that very spot. It sounded like a giant redwood had just crashed to the ground. My dad, the tree killer.

Lesson #5 – I don't know. Go green? Plant a tree.

Thanks Dad!

CECELIA

She grew up near Pittsburgh.

Her parents divorced when she was only ten.

She lived with her dad.

In high school, she was a cheerleader.

After graduating, she worked in a grocery store.

When she met the guy she'd later marry, a tall, lanky Maryland farm boy, she was already engaged to someone else.

She said "I do" a few months shy of her 21st birthday. He was 24, fresh out of the Army.

They lived in Pennsylvania, Ohio for a year, and then Pennsylvania.

She had two sons, the first when she was 26 and the second almost five years later.

Her home was the cleanest around.

When her youngest was in high school, she decided to show houses instead of clean them and got her real estate license.

She was my mother.

Not my mom, or mum.

"A mum is a flower!" she'd say. "I'm your mother!"

As a little boy, I remember "lovin' time" when I'd curl up with her on the couch before bedtime.

My dad traveled a lot for his job and she was in charge.

She was strict, but fair.

She wasn't all that happy when I poured extra salt on her plate of spaghetti to see if she'd notice. She noticed all right, but didn't care for the joke.

She was a good cook. I can see the stainless steel pot of chili simmering on the stove and remember how I'd look forward to that night's dinner. And those melt in your mouth shortbread cookies that were sooooo good.

She was thin but loved her chocolate M&M's® and could take on a large bag in one setting. Just like me.

She fought Hodgkin's Disease when I was twelve or thirteen. My dad would bring her home from chemotherapy and she'd go straight to bed, sick from the nausea. The next morning, she'd be up, cleaning the house. She'd win that battle, but not a later one with lung cancer.

She loved her coffee and cigarettes which she started smoking as a teenager. When I was in high school, we argued about those damn cigarettes.

When her mother gave in to alcohol, and tried to take her own life, my mother moved her back from Florida so that she and her sister could watch over her.

She was a regular at the local Bob Evans® restaurant.

She loved Whoopi Goldberg in the movie *Sister Act*.

She was a proud woman, always wanting to look her best and got her hair done every Friday morning.

She was a fighter. Stubborn. Determined. Strong-willed. Just like her sons.

She had her idiosyncrasies, like pulling in the driveway, opening the garage door and then backing up to straighten out the car before pulling in. She did it every time, even though the car was already straight. It drove me crazy.

She loved her two grandsons and they loved their 'Grammy'. She'd be proud of them today, all grown up with families of their own.

It's hard to believe she passed almost 16 years ago.

Happy Mother's Day mom.

I mean, Mother.

☺

■ ■ ■

As the baby, of course I was her favorite.

A LITTLE CORN, A LOTTA TEARS AND ONE BIG BROTHER TO THE RESCUE

From the time I was little, I learned real fast I'd never be a good criminal. On a chilly October night, when I was about six, I was tick tacking with my brother and some of his friends.

That's what you did in the weeks leading up to Halloween. Armed with a sack of field corn, you'd wait until after dark and then prowl the neighborhood. When you saw lights on in a house, and maybe even people in their living room watching television, you'd reach into your sack of corn and let a handful fly, aiming at the window, hopefully scaring the pumpkin out of them. At that point, you'd run and hide. And wait. If you were lucky, the man of the house would come flying out the front door cussing at you.

Other than a good scare, no one got hurt and no windows were broken. It was all in fun.

As long as everything went as planned.

On this particular October night, we were doing our thing. Only five minutes from home, and a few streets away, we picked our next target, threw our corn and took off into the night. And just as we'd hoped, the front door flew open and Mr. Grumpy Old Man came out yelling.

"You dang kids! I oughta kick your @@$#!"

Success.

But then something happened that wasn't supposed to.

He caught me.

At six years old, you can only run so fast. I don't remember if I hid too close to the house or what. All I know is that he was holding on to me by the collar of my shirt and I wasn't getting away.

This was not good. According to my brother, that's when things really took a turn for the worse.

"Jooooohn!" I cried out as tears ran down my face. "He got me. Jooooohn!"

I obviously hadn't learned an important lesson. In covert missions like this, you don't rat out your accomplices. If caught, you go down alone.

To a scared six year old, that didn't make a lot of sense. The only thing I cared about at that moment was seeing my big brother.

"You'd better come and get him!" yelled Mr. Grumpy Old Man.

I was in complete agreement. My brother had better come and get me.

"Jooooohn!"

Reluctantly, and knowing he had little choice, my big brother appeared out of the darkness to save me. I appreciated the gesture. But come on? What would he have said to our parents if he hadn't?

"If you want him back, the guy on the corner of Colonial and Northumberland has him."

That wouldn't have gone over too well with my mother. I don't think so anyway.

I don't recall much about the particulars of my release, but I know I slept in my own bed that night. I would live to see another day. As long as my brother didn't kill me before then.

That incident marked the end of my tick tacking career. I don't think I got to hang around with my brother and his friends too much after that either.

When I look back on it now, it wasn't such a bad thing. I only had to mow the guy's lawn a few times. At least I didn't have to paint his windows.

My brother got stuck with that.

WISH YOU WERE HERE

Whenever we travel, I see postcards for sale. In the airport, in shops, all the usual places.

Even in this world of emails, texts, tweets and selfies, I guess I'm not the only one who still sends them.

Do you?

A lady I used to work with sent me one from Africa when she was there on a safari. That was cool. Until I realized she wrote most of it before she ever left her house. You could tell from the way she worded it.

Thanks.

You shouldn't have.

Really.

Almost thirty years ago, we were in Florida with friends. Stan and I were admiring the postcards of scantily clad women when my wife asked what we were doing.

Thinking quickly, as guys do in those situations, I said, "We're looking for something for Wes."

"Yeah, that's it," Stan agreed.

My wife wasn't buying it, especially since Wes, my nephew, was only three at the time.

And from that point on, Stan and I would send each other 'Wes postcards'.

Poor Wes. He never did see one.

Last week I sent a postcard to my cousin.

He's on vacation.

He got a laugh out of that.

So did I.

When we go away, I take my address list and postcard stamps with us. One name that's no longer on that list is my aunt's, the only one I ever had. She passed away last December.

In her 83 years on this earth, my aunt Loretta rarely ventured far from her home in western Pennsylvania. She did go to Florida once at Christmas with her husband and two youngest to visit her mom, my grandmother. I remember how surprised we all were that she was going. And she once said she'd never been west of Ohio. She didn't have to travel far to see her five kids and their families because they all lived nearby.

A few years back, she surprised us again when she went on a multi-day trip to Smith Mountain Lake in southern Virginia with a friend and his family. Obviously, she was getting wild and adventurous in her older age.

On their way home, they stopped at our house for lunch. That's when I saw something I thought I never would. My aunt in my house. After all, we lived in Virginia, four hours away from her. We teased her about it and all got a good laugh. I have the pictures to prove she was here.

I don't remember for sure, but I think I started sending her postcards as a way to show her how much world was out there. I wouldn't tell her when we were going, or where. I wanted to surprise her. She liked getting those postcards and told us she'd kept them all. She even pulled out the stack to show us.

I was impressed.

We're going on vacation soon and I'm looking forward to it. But when I realized I wouldn't be sending her a postcard this time, or ever again, I was bummed.

Maybe I'll send her one anyway.

Aunt Loretta, I really do 'wish you were here'.

■ ■ ■

Christmas wasn't Christmas without her shortbread cookies. Mmm mmm.

KIND WORDS

She leaned toward me as she approached, smiled and whispered "I liked your article."

Surprised, I looked up and returned the smile.

"Thanks."

Every other Sunday morning, on her way to communion, she'd touch my arm or shoulder and say that.

Ok, not every other Sunday. Only when my article was good.

I looked forward to those little encounters. They brightened my day. Who doesn't like to hear kind words?

One Sunday morning, before heading to my usual seat, she handed me a bulletin and laughed.

"I want to meet your wife."

And recently, when Judy joined me in Church, she did.

Two months ago, before the service started, she handed me a card and said "Happy Birthday", again catching me off guard.

I took the card and laughed.

"How did she know?" I wondered, and then remembered the church keeps a list of everyone's birthday.

An unexpected gesture, and one that made my special day a bit more special.

A few weeks ago, I saw her do the same thing to a woman who was sitting across the aisle from me.

I didn't know Betty all that well, but from what I've heard the past few days, those were the kind of things she was always doing for others.

When I opened my email early this past Sunday morning and quickly scanned the list of unread messages, one from the Church caught my eye.

I didn't like the title. "Some Sad News".

When I opened it and saw Betty's name, I didn't want to believe it was true.

But it was.

She'd passed away the day before.

And then I remembered I hadn't seen her in Church the previous Sunday. She was always in Church.

A few weeks after she gave me that birthday card, I called the Church office to find out when hers was.

"May 23rd," the secretary said without even having to look it up.

I marked the date on my calendar. I'd be sure to wish Betty a happy birthday next year, and maybe surprise her.

Sadly, I won't get to do that.

There are people we meet on our life's journey who we wish we'd gotten to know better.

Betty was one of those people.

When I began writing my "Engle's Angle" column more than seven years ago, I put together a list of email addresses for family and friends who didn't live in the area. Every other Friday, when the paper hit the newsstands, I'd send my article to everyone on that list.

I was excited to add readers in new states.

"I now have one in Illinois and Colorado!" I'd tell my wife.

When I heard the news about Betty, I knew I had one in Heaven too.

I hope she'll keep reading it.

And put a good word in for me as well.

THE LEGEND OF THE GREAT WHITE GHOST

One October night,
many moons ago,
a group of boys
got a horrible fright.
Here's how so.

Out on the streets
we'd choose our target.
On the count of three
we'd let it fly.
A handful of corn
into the night sky.

Rattling on house windows,
scaring those inside.
We'd run off into the night
laughing with pride.

When we'd finished
with our mischief and fun,
it was time to go home.
For tonight,
our work was done.

As we walked up the road
toward our houses,
none of us knew
what was lurking around us.

All of a sudden, he appeared.
Jumping out of the bushes,
screaming bloody murder,
the Great White Ghost
would let us go no further.

We yelled and scattered
as quickly as we could.
All but one
whose legs were like wood

He alone remained
before the Great White Ghost.
His legs buckled.
He fell to his feet.
On the ground,
passed out on the street.

It was Danny or Brian.
I don't remember.
But when he came to,
he was cryin'.

Standing six foot two,
the Great White Ghost
was someone
we all knew.

For when he removed
his white sheet,
my own dad
was underneath.

Years later,
we still recall that night.
When, as kids,
we got a horrible fright.

So be on the lookout this Halloween
for ghosts and goblins
and all scary things
in between.

PART EIGHT

A Special Time Of Year

THE WORST GIFT EVER?

My wife is amazing. Each year at Christmas, she always knows what to get for everyone. But how does she do it? By doing something that I don't. She pays attention. She notices what people like, what they eat, what they enjoy doing. Me? I'm clueless. I don't even know what to tell Santa Claus to bring me.

But one year, she messed up. One Christmas, she got it all wrong. And the worst part of it? It was for me. Her own husband. How could she? Of course, being the nice guy I am, I remind her about it every year.

That was the year she got me something I didn't want, didn't need and would never use. That was the year she got me the worst gift ever. A wooden flute.

Just saying it sounds strange. Who buys a flute for someone at Christmas?

Ok, let's back up for a minute. In my wife's defense, she knows I love music. I enjoy going to concerts and always have the radio on. But that's where it ends. I can't sing and I have absolutely no musical talent. Two facts she's well aware of. One of my nephews plays the guitar and another the drums. I've strummed that guitar and beat on those drums, but anyone who's heard it, including my wife, knows the result was anything but musical. When I was a kid, my parents never took me for any type of music lessons. Somehow they knew it wasn't in my future.

My wife chose to ignore all of this and buy the flute anyway. She saw it at a holiday craft show. For about 25 bucks, I was about to become the owner of my very own flute. To this day, she still can't give me a good reason why.

When I opened the box, my reaction was a bit less than enthusiastic. No doubt you've received one of those presents too.

"Thanks," I said out of politeness, knowing that I didn't really mean it.

"What the heck is this?" is what was actually going through my mind at the time, as well as "Huh?"

As expected, my initial attempts to play it were not very successful. To be honest, there weren't many attempts after that. In fact, that flute hasn't seen much daylight in the 10 years or so since I got it.

I've always thought that was the worst $25 my wife ever spent. But as time goes by, I realize I was wrong. Every time I think about that wooden flute, and every time we talk about it, we laugh. I still don't know how to play the darned thing and doubt that I ever will. It hasn't produced much music in its day, but it has generated a lot of laughs. And for 25 bucks, that's not bad.

ALL THAT GLITTERS

Answer:

A. You don't want them in your underwear.
B. You shouldn't eat them.
C. You'll find them everywhere.
D. All of the above.

Question: What do sand, artificial Christmas tree needles and glitter have in common?

What were we thinking? Obviously we weren't. What other reasonable explanation could there be? Why else would we buy Christmas cards with glitter on them? I hate glitter. It gets in everything and on everything. Like sand from the beach that you find months after your summer vacation, and artificial Christmas tree needles that mysteriously keep appearing long after the holidays are over, the same is true of glitter. And once it gets on you or your clothes, it's there for life.

When it was time to write our cards and I opened the first of three boxes, I was not happy. We don't like *receiving* glitter-filled

272 KEVIN S. ENGLE

cards. Why did we *buy* them? No matter who was to blame, although I think my wife was the guilty party, immediate action was required. Carefully handling them, as if they were radioactive waste, I had to contain the mess to one location. Get out a beach towel, check for sand, and go to work. It was a good idea. Good ideas don't always work.

These cards weren't sprinkled with glitter. They were doused with it. Drenched. Soaked. Saturated. You get the idea. There was so much on the inside of the cards that it rendered my pen useless after just a few times signing them. Even the envelopes were full of it. We couldn't lick them unless we wanted shiny tongues. My wife suggested using a wet sponge to seal them. It worked, but that meant glitter in the kitchen. The stuff was already spreading like an out-of-control computer virus.

We spread out our Christmas card writing over several days. When we were done each night, I'd roll up the towel to quarantine the little things, and then off we'd go to the hose down station to wash away the radioactive debris from our clothes and bodies.

When the cards were ready to mail, into a plastic bag they went. I didn't want it all over the inside of my car, but I'm sure it's just a matter of time before I start spotting it there too.

I'm getting a little smarter, not as though that's saying much. Now I open all our cards over the garbage can in case they contain you know what. And if they do, I've been known to utter a nasty word or two.

Answer:

A. Postal workers were required to warn recipients of incoming hazardous material. "Warning – Glitter" should do the trick.

B. Glitter manufacturers were fined for littering. After all, it is G + litter.

C. I hit the lottery.

D. All of the above

Question: The world would be a better place if

NO THANKS. JUST LOOKING.

"Hello sir! How are you today?"

"Oh great," I muttered to myself. "Here we go."

"Fine," I replied without making eye contact. I had barely stepped in the store when she pounced.

"Is there anything I can help you find today?"

"Yeah, someplace where you won't bother me." Wouldn't it be nice to say what you were *really* thinking? Of course I didn't and gave her the standard reply.

"No thanks. Just looking," I said as I veered away from her, doing my best avoidance move.

"If you need anything, my name is Kris. Just like Kris Kringle." And then she laughed, although it sounded more like a snort, something a reindeer would do.

There are two kinds of shoppers. Those who don't mind being helped by a sales associate, and people like me. The ones who don't want to be bothered. Leave me alone, and IF I have a question, I'll ask. That's why I hate car shopping. You can't do it without being pestered. Today looked to be heading down the same path.

I didn't tell Kris the truth. I wasn't just looking. I was on a mission. I was Christmas shopping for my wife. I was in search of two items, one that I already knew I wanted, and a second mystery gift. I can't be any more specific than that, or you know who might know you know what.

Somehow, I found item #1 right away, as if it drew me to it like a magnet. But all was not well.

Have you ever had that feeling someone is right behind you? Kris was hovering.

"Oh yes, that's very nice," she gushed. "I really like that too. I've had my eye on those."

I looked around the store. I was the only customer there. Not good. For me or the store. No one else for Kris to "help".

"I'm curious to see if you pick the one I like best," she said.

"Oh me too. The suspense is just killing me," I wanted to say. But of course, I didn't. I smiled half heartedly and walked away. I had to buy a second item for my coupon to kick in. I circled the store, hoping something would catch my eye. Nothing did.

On my second pass, I heard the most wonderful sound imaginable. The ringing of the bell above the store entrance. And a second later, "Hello ladies, how are you? Can I help you find anything today?"

"Hallelujah!" I cried out.

A few minutes later, after I'd found something I thought my wife would like, I returned to item #1. And guess who was waiting for me?

There were several to pick from. Narrowing my choices to the two I liked best, I made my selection.

"That's the one I preferred," she said. "Excellent choice. Is there anything else you need today?"

"Some ear plugs maybe?"

I grunted "no" and headed toward the counter. While some-one else rang up the sale, Kris circled back to her next victims.

After paying, I grabbed the bag and quickly headed for the door.

"Thank you sir and Happy Holidays!" she called out. "If you need a new car, my husband sells those."

I should've known.

ALL I WANT FOR CHRISTMAS

All I want for Christmas

. . . are clothes. Nice clothes. Clothes I like. But my wife won't get them for me. Why? Because she's Scrooge? Or the Grinch? No. She doesn't buy me clothes. She used to, but says I'm too picky. I'd always take them back and exchange them for ones I liked better. Why waste her time she says. She's got a point.

Last year I asked for the perfect present. A gift card from my favorite men's clothing store. I could get anything I wanted, and it was already paid for. What could be better than that? I knew I'd see that under the tree. I never did find it. My wife doesn't do gift cards.

All I want for Christmas

. . . is candy. Butterfingers®, Toblerone®, Heath® Bars. All my favorites. I doubt that's gonna happen either. My sweet wife says I can buy that stuff anytime. True, but it'd sure be nice if I found some in my stocking.

All I want for Christmas

. . . are DVDs of several movies I really enjoyed. My wife says I don't like to watch movies that I've already seen. True, I don't like to watch them ten times in a row like little kids do, but I would like to add a few to our collection. And I will. When I buy them myself.

All I want for Christmas

… is a chainsaw, but sure as Santa lives at the North Pole, I won't be getting one. I've never owned a chainsaw. I need a chainsaw. It'd be a lot faster than my handsaw. My wife says they're too dangerous. She says I'd hurt myself. She's probably right. Correction. She is right. Maybe I don't really want a chainsaw after all.

All I want for Christmas

… are tickets to some baseball games next summer. My wife doesn't like to plan that far ahead. "When the time comes," she'll say, "we might want to do something else." Looks like that idea was a strike out.

All I want for Christmas

… is a wide brimmed hat to protect my head from the sun. But it can't be dweeby or nerdy or goofy looking. She says I already have a wide brimmed hat. I do, but it scratches my bald head and doesn't block out the sun all that well. If my wife really cared about me, and my head, she'd get it. But she won't. She'll say I need to pick that out myself, just like my clothes.

All I want for Christmas

… is my two front teeth. And I'm gonna need them after my wife reads this. Oh well, at least I'll get something I want. For once.

Merry Cwithmuth evwybody!

THE SOUNDS OF THE SEASON.
THE SOUNDS OF THE SEASON. THE
SOUNDS OF THE SEASON.

Repeat after me.

I love Christmas music. I love Christmas music. I love Christmas music.

I do. Especially in December. But that's not when it begins. With Black Friday shopping starting sometime in October, the "sounds of the season" kick off soon after that.

As much as I love those holiday songs, by the time December 25th gets here, I'm as tired of them as Santa is after a night of delivering toys.

This year, after listening to those tunes for hours on end, here's what I know:

- Grandma's been run over by a reindeer so many times she's as flat as one week old road kill.
- I rocked around the Christmas tree so much I got motion sickness.
- and thanks to "Feliz Navidad" and "O Tannenbaum", I'm now fluent in Spanish and German.

Have you ever seen a TV commercial so many times that you quit paying attention to it and still don't know what it's advertising? That's me and "The 12 Days of Christmas". If I had to name all 12 days correctly before getting my presents, I wouldn't be getting any presents. Ever.

And if Santa Claus is comin' to town, is he ever gonna get here? How long does it take? He's been doing it enough years that he must know the way by now. At the very least, you'd think the Mrs. would've gotten him a nice GPS for the sleigh.

And despite all the radio stations playing Christmas music every minute of every day, there really are only 10 different holiday songs and you hear them over and over and over. Anyone who can sing has recorded his or her own Christmas CD with those 10 songs on it. Even if you can't sing, it doesn't matter. For instance, the dogs who bark "Jingle Bells". I have to admit they are pretty good.

Plus, if you're popular, and you've been nice, you're guaranteed to have your own holiday TV show. On the other hand, if you've been naughty, you'll only get to make a guest appearance on somebody else's show.

I can't even get away from the music by turning off the radio and TV. I've heard those songs so often they're stuck in my head. I caught myself humming "Let it Snow" in the shower the other day.

> But here's the weird part. When Christmas is over,
>   so is the music.
> It's gone.
> Just like that.
> A true Silent Night.
> They get me addicted to the music, and then they
>   cut me off.

And I miss it.

I can't go cold turkey just like that. I don't even like cold turkey.

Before I know it, it's New Year's Eve and time for "Auld Lang Syne."

There's another song I'll never know the words too.

At least I only have to hear that for a day or two.

UNDERWEAR > IPAD

My wife handed me two packages on Christmas morning.

"Open this one first," she said. "I got the second one just in case."

I didn't like the sound of that.

"An iPad," I announced, as if she didn't already know what it was. And as she had correctly anticipated, I was about as happy as if she'd just given me a bushel sack of lima beans.

"Ok, now this one."

"Underwear." I was a bit more enthused. It was on my list. An iPad wasn't.

It's now three weeks later. I'm wearing my underwear. I haven't opened the iPad. And I don't intend to. As soon as I can wrestle the receipt away from my wife, it's going back.

Like Crest toothpaste, three out of four dentists, and non-dentists, think I'm nuts. But I've given this a lot of thought. I can now say, without a doubt, that underwear > iPad.

Here's why.

First of all, it's a lot cheaper. Do you know how much underwear you could buy for what an iPad costs? A lot.

Secondly, underwear works anywhere, not just in certain places. You put it on and it does what it does, and we all know what that is. The iPad, on the other hand, only works in *special* places. Places with WiFi. No WiFi, no iPad. That is, unless you want to pay the phone company extra each month for that capability. With my underwear, that's not an issue. With WiFi, I'm good. Without WiFi, still good. And no extra charges. I don't have to pay the phone company or anybody else to make sure my underwear is working properly. And that's important. Like a loyal pet, it's always there to support me.

Thirdly, I don't need any instructions telling me how to set up my underwear or make them work. Wash and wear. With an iPad, it's not that simple. Although from what I've heard, these things don't even come with instructions. You're supposed to magically know how to make them work. Un huh.

If I take care of my underwear and treat it right, which I plan to, we'll have a long lasting relationship. Several years at least. With the iPad, I've gotta worry about not dropping it. Someone stealing it. Me losing it. All kinds of stuff that I don't want to think about. And what's more, my underwear will still be as effective a few years from now as it was on Day 1. I don't have to be concerned with software glitches, identity theft or buying the newest model. Underwear 1.0 will be just fine.

From what I've been told, you can do some neat stuff with an iPad. But can it be more important than what underwear does? I don't think so. Unless you're one of those people who don't wear any. Then you don't care.

Maybe that's it. Maybe all the people who use iPads don't wear underwear? Hmmm.

You can have your iPad. I'll keep my underwear.

WINE AND WHINE

Every Christmas, my wife and I exchange gifts with our brothers and their families. I have one and she has three.

Some years, we just can't figure out what to get them. And when we do, we still have to pack it up and ship it out. Not a cheap thing these days.

This year, I just wasn't in the mood to come up with that perfect gift. Or any gift for that matter.

My wife and I talked and decided now was the time. The subject had come up before, but we'd never done anything about it. It was time to take a stand.

I typed the email and hit "send".

"Are you guys ok with not exchanging Christmas gifts anymore?" I asked softly. "We're looking for ways to simplify the Holidays and eliminate some of the stress."

And that's the truth. I don't like shopping to begin with. And when I have no clue what to buy, it's even worse.

But I wasn't being totally honest. I wasn't really *asking* if it was ok. I was telling them that's what we were going to do, like it or not.

Don't get me wrong. I enjoy getting gifts and I enjoy giving gifts. But sometimes, you get to a point where it's not fun anymore. And that's where we were.

The responses came back quickly and were what we'd hoped for. Except one.

"Told you so," my wife said. She saw this coming.

Nothing is simple with this guy. Some people just cannot give you a yes or no. They have to go on. And on. My two sentence email resulted in a full page reply which went something like this:

"Sure, if that's what you want to do, but don't ask us to stop giving you a gift. That's being a real Scrooge. After all, this is a special time of year when we should stop and think of others who are important in our lives."

Yeah, yeah, whatever.

He concluded with "it's still not too late to get us a bottle of wine from that place we really like."

Is that so? The truth comes out.

Having initiated this whole thing, I did what any intelligent guy would do.

I let my wife get back to him.

After all, it was her brother.

The more I thought about what he said, the worse I felt. I didn't want to be a Scrooge. And I do think it's important to think about those who mean the most to us, and not just at this time of year.

The next day, I took his suggestion and got that bottle of wine.

And you can be sure I'll say a toast to him when we pop the cork.

■ ■ ■

A toast. "Drink wine. Don't whine." Happy Holidays!

PINK PIGS AND SUPER-SIZED SANTAS

Several Decembers ago, I decided to decorate outside for the holidays. I'd never done it before.

Knowing full well the limit of my skills and intelligence for projects like these, not to mention my patience, I would take it slowly.

We have two pine trees in the front yard. I'd start with those and see how that went. Putting lights on the house itself was beyond my talents.

Before I could put up lights, I needed to buy lights. But how many? I didn't have a clue. Outside extension cords as well.

For the first two years, I didn't use a timer. Having to go outside and unplug those lights each night got old, and cold, real fast.

When I did get timers, I purchased two. The simple made-for-me model, and the more complex read-the-directions-to-figure-it-out kind. That one still confuses me.

To put up the lights, I needed a ladder. To do the job without getting dizzy, I needed several ladders so that I wouldn't have to keep moving it around the tree every ten seconds.

I also didn't realize you need to know which end of the lights to start with. That would be the 'female' receptor end. That way when you get to the bottom of the tree and need to plug the lights in to an extension cord, you can. I have to think that through every year. This project requires a degree in Electrical Engineering. Something I don't have.

And you don't just throw the lights on the tree. How tightly are you supposed to wrap them around the tree? My wife and I always disagree about that one. "Don't choke it," she'll say.

Flash ahead to this December. Those pine trees that I could easily reach the top of that first year have gotten bigger. My ladder isn't tall enough anymore. Now I'd need a high lift to do the job.

And a basic fact of Christmas tree lights is they burn out.

Some of mine only lasted one season. They were guaranteed for three.

I returned them a time or two to the manufacturer but had to pay for the shipping and that wasn't cheap. I might as well buy new.

I now have several strands where ½ the lights work and the other ½ doesn't. Being the cheapo I am, you don't throw those away. So, using two of those strands, and positioning them correctly, you can't even tell when the sun goes down and the lights come on.

My neighbor across the street said they look nice, and they must, because if they didn't, she'd say so. She decorates one in her front yard as well and then leaves it lit for months. It looks good. In December. But not so much in February.

I love Christmas trees. But not in February.

And last year, another neighbor put up one of those inflatable Santas in his front yard. Ol' Saint Nick must be twelve foot tall. He scared me the first time I saw him.

I was driving around doing errands a couple days ago when I spotted two pink pigs on the roof of someone's house. I'm not sure what pink pigs have to do with Christmas, but ok, whatever.

Pink pigs and Super-Sized Santas.

'Tis the season.

■ ■ ■

The author would like to borrow Super-Sized Santa. Ol' Saint Nick could reach the top of those pine trees.

Made in the USA
San Bernardino, CA
30 November 2017